THE GRAD'S GUIDE TO

SURVIVING STRESSFUL TIMES

NAVPRESS

Discipleship Inside Out™

THINK

NavPress is the publishing ministry of The Navigators, an international Christian organization and leader in personal spiritual development. NavPress is committed to helping people grow spiritually and enjoy lives of meaning and hope through personal and group resources that are biblically rooted, culturally relevant, and highly practical.

For a free catalog go to www.NavPress.com
or call 1.800.366.7788 in the United States or 1.800.839.4769 in Canada.

© 2011 by The Navigators

All rights reserved. No part of this publication may be reproduced in any form without written permission from NavPress, P.O. Box 35001, Colorado Springs, CO 80935. www.navpress.com

NAVPRESS and the NAVPRESS logo are registered trademarks of NavPress. Absence of ® in connection with marks of NavPress or other parties does not indicate an absence of registration of those marks.

ISBN-13: 978-1-61521-607-9

Cover design by Arvid Wallen
Cover photo by lightpoet, Shutterstock Images LLC

Produced with the assistance of The Livingstone Corporation (www.livingstonecorp.com). Project staff included Neil Wilson.

Some of the anecdotal illustrations in this book are true to life and are included with the permission of the persons involved. All other illustrations are composites of real situations, and any resemblance to people living or dead is coincidental.

Unless otherwise identified, all Scripture quotations in this publication are taken from *THE MESSAGE* (MSG). Copyright © 1993, 1994, 1995, 1996, 2000, 2001, 2002. Used by permission of NavPress Publishing Group. Other versions used include: the *Holy Bible, New International Version*® (NIV®), Copyright © 1973, 1978, 1984 by International Bible Society, used by permission of Zondervan, all rights reserved.

Library of Congress Cataloging-in-Publication Data

The grad's guide to surviving stressful times.
    p. cm.
 "TH1NK."
 ISBN 978-1-61521-607-9
 1. Christian college students--Religious life. 2. Stress
(Psychology)--Religious aspects--Christianity.
 BV4531.3.G71 2010
 248.8'34--dc22

                            2010040279

Printed in the United States of America

1 2 3 4 5 6 7 8 / 15 14 13 12 11

Contents

INTRODUCTION/WELCOME

Welcome to *The Grad's Guide to Surviving Stressful Times*. Now, you may be wishing you had gotten this a few months ago, before the graduation grind really began, but it's never too late to start making sense of everything that life has suddenly decided to dump on you. This is about *survival*.

Then again, you may be thinking, *Stress? What stress? My world is good and life is great! I'm not having any stress!* If this is your current experience, we say, "Enjoy it while it lasts." The fact that you are not feeling any stress may well be because, for the moment, your life is completely in order; your plans are set; and no one has decided that their ideas about your future are more significant than your plans. In case that changes sometime in the near future, keep this book close.

Or you may be in complete denial and just not recognize your level of stress. In which case we suggest this book might really come in handy. Not only will it give you some ideas about handling stressful times, but it may help you recognize feelings or responses you didn't realize are actually the results of stress.

So, let's talk a little about stressful times. What is stress? Stress is anything you feel that relates to what's beyond your control. We'll talk more about this along the way, but you can often feel stressed when you get that sneaky sense there's more going on than you can handle. If it's bigger than you, it can cause stress. If the situation requires more time, more wisdom, more money, more strength, or more of just about anything else, the result inside you can be *stress*.

One of the surprising discoveries people make when they begin to learn about stress is that stress can come from good experiences just as often as it comes from bad times. Losing a job can create a lot of stress, but so can getting a better job with more responsibility, especially if you will have to move across the country to take the new position. Getting married is one of the really great experiences in life, but it can also bring with it loads of stress. Who knew that a one-day celebration could deliver such a mind-boggling accumulation of decisions, most of which involve someone spending money.

Now, getting a job or getting married may well be on your list of *things way down the road of life*, but every stage of growth, particularly as you enter adulthood, comes with its own collection of stress-inducing highs and lows. Think of this book as a friendly heads-up from people who may have gotten decked by stress and want to give you a chance to avoid the headaches.

The last thing we want to do is make reading this book stressful. One of the first things that disappear from a person's life in stressful times is the capacity for laughter. Losing your smile and forgetting how to laugh are clues that you're under a significant amount of stress. But laughter is a good stress buster. So, here's our first memo for action: Keep track of the movies and comedians that really make you laugh. Build a small collection of these components as a "stress first-aid kit." Remember, good, healthy comedy makes you laugh over and over, not just one time—fill your emergency kit with examples of persistent humor. Then take time to rerun those funny scenes and let yourself laugh. Next to praying, laughing in the middle of stressful times is a healthy approach to living.

We intend to make *The Grad's Guide to Surviving Stressful Times* an enjoyable, and perhaps occasionally even a humorous, experience for you. Stress itself is no laughing matter, but a smile or a chuckle may actually make you feel better than two aspirin when it comes to dealing with stressful times. The wisdom that comes from God's Word will allow you to step back with relief because you know Someone who is bigger than anything life throws at you.

1

The Calm Before the Stress
(Meeting Some Stress Survivors)

L ike lots of young people, Dan was looking forward to leaving home. Just a few more years in prep school and he'd be done. Even his advanced classes hadn't been all that difficult, and Dan thought maybe it was time to take on something a little more challenging. He and his friends spent a lot of time talking about the future and wondering where they would be in ten years. The possibilities were exciting. But first, things needed to get wrapped up at home.

Dan was liked by his peers even though he wasn't a star athlete, and he didn't get fame on campus by strange behavior. In fact, he seemed like a normal kid growing up in his time. He had three close friends he'd known all his life, and they gradually formed a tight circle of commitment that would last a lifetime.

Although people watching from the outside could tell these

four guys had a strong friendship, very few understood the cause. But Dan and his friends knew exactly the special bond they shared. Sure, they had a lot of experiences in common and their education was identical. Their families were from the same neighborhood and knew each other well. The boys had their share of adventures—you know, the kind of death-defying stuff you do as a child that you don't get around to telling your parents about because you know you'll never do *that* again. Eventually, you discover that your parents have their own set of stupid and silly growing-up tricks that they also survived. Beyond all these rites of passage, Dan and his friends had a deeper bond.

Somewhere around junior high age, the four boys got serious about God. It was a lot more than deciding to go to church together or be part of the same youth group. Do you know how unusual it is for four friends (especially guys) to sit around and talk about God? It wasn't even an official Bible study, but these friends decided together that whatever else came along in life, they were going to live for God. They even got comfortable having lengthy conversations together with God—the four of them, sitting in a quiet place and talking to a fifth person who couldn't be seen, but seemed to be *there* with them, listening.

Funny thing is, almost everyone wants to have relationships like Dan had with his friends. Most of us want to have a level of connection with a few other people that involves everything in life, including God. We don't want to have to always edit what we think and say. We want to know we're with other people who share the same "most important stuff" with us. Yet most of us also end up settling for surface friendships that never really go deep. We don't get to know each other. Most of the stuff we spend time thinking about we never tell our friends because we don't trust them or know them well enough. But we wish we could tell them, and we wish we did trust them.

So, why don't we? Why don't we know others deeply? Why don't we let others know us? Mostly it's fear. We don't want to risk the first step because we might be walking off a cliff. We're afraid of what might happen if we say to our friends, "What about taking our conversations to a deeper level?" We imagine that look in their eyes, or the pulling away, or even a comment like "What are you talking about?" We are all waiting for someone else to take the risk. But sometimes, if we really want the rich reward of deeper friendships, we have to run the risk of opening up.

That's what happened with Dan and his friends. Looking back, no one remembered who made the first move, but all of them immediately agreed that deeper was a direction they wanted to go. Although each had been thinking a lot about God recently, they all admitted that until that point no one had really brought up "The Big One" in regular conversation. They had certainly heard sermons and teaching about God from adults and had participated in official discussions, but deciding for themselves to talk about God as part of their friendship was a new adventure. One of their early discoveries was that all of them had pretty much the same questions about God and that when they pursued answers together, they usually made more progress than when they were thinking alone. And when they looked for answers in God's Word, well, four heads were better than one. The lessons they learned together and the conclusions they reached by helping each other cemented their relationship.

As the time for the next level of education appeared on the horizon, Dan was excited about the possibilities. The four guys thought they might even go on to college together. But there was war in the Middle East at the time, and Dan was aware that he might be called up for duty if it went on much longer. Dan's family was connected and well-off, but there was still a chance he would have to serve in the military, especially if the war escalated. Along with his friends, Dan was obviously officer material, and if the army called, they would step up to serve.

Up to this point in his life, Dan had lived a relatively stress-free existence. Like most people in their adolescent years, Dan had his share of crushes, drama, and crises, but he managed the side effects of these years without lasting problems. His worries never caused him to break a sweat, and even though the future was a little uncertain, Dan was confident that God had things under control. As events unfolded around him, it is clear that Dan learned some crucial lessons early in life that prepared him for the stormy stress that followed the calm of his childhood. Although Dan eventually demonstrated a unique, God-given capacity for understanding future events, there's no hint from his childhood that he realized how far from home his commitment to God would eventually take him and his friends.

The same lessons Dan learned we want to share with you as we look at some of the potential "stressors" heading your way in the years to come. Hopefully, you won't have to immediately apply all of these insights. This is supposed to be a gift of preparation not a crisis intervention. Some of our examples may differ from your actual experiences. But everything that Dan learned and applied to his life is worth knowing. You probably won't face exactly the same challenges and obstacles he faced, but Dan's pattern and the strategies he and his friends used will work in your life, too. We know this, not only because we have tested these principles ourselves and watched them prove true in other lives but also because these principles come from God's Word. That's where we meet the actual Dan, or Daniel (as his mother always called him), and his three friends: Hananiah, Mishael, and Azariah. Their story is told in the book of Daniel in the Old Testament, and he is mentioned several other key places in the Bible.

Can you imagine having three friends with names like the guys who hung out with Daniel? The first thing you'd want to do is give them each a nickname. You'd probably call them Han, Mish, and Az for short. Well, these four friends were eagerly anticipating graduation day. They were ready for the excitement of life on their own. But what they got instead was a disaster—and a sudden world of stress in their lives.

Panic in the Promised Land

Sometimes you can see stress-producing events coming a mile away; other times they pop up like the bad guys in a suspense movie who make you jump before you can even tell what's about to happen. For Dan, Han, Mish, and Az, stress showed up like a bad storm when their king was killed in battle and their country was conquered. Almost overnight things went from normal to chaos in the people's lives. Suddenly, the future was up for grabs. We don't know how much Dan and his friends were aware of everything that was going on, but we can make some educated guesses about the way things looked from their point of view as young people. They were part of a society going through turmoil at several different crucial levels. Things were a mess spiritually, morally, and politically. But in order to understand what Dan and his friends faced, we must step back a little further in time.

A Godly Ruler

During most of their childhood, Dan and his friends were aware of an amazing king who reigned in Judah. His name was King Josiah. His face was probably on the boxes of cereal at the breakfast table. He was the talk of the town. During a time when kings were mostly famous for being as rotten as possible, Josiah stood out as the right kind of leader, good to the bone.

Part of Josiah's hero story was the fact that he became king of Judah when he was just eight years old. Not bad — in elementary school one day and absolutely biggest man on campus the next. When you get that much power at such a young age, it's hard to predict how you will turn out.

Josiah's grandfather was Manasseh, one of the worst kings Judah ever had. Like Josiah, Manasseh came to the throne young — only twelve. The fifty-five years that Manasseh ruled in Jerusalem created complete havoc in the spiritual lives of the people. There was a lot of religious stuff going on, much like there is today, but almost all of it had to do with people satisfying their most evil and cruel desires and putting religious labels on it. As the Bible puts it, "In GOD's judgment he was a bad king—an evil king. He reintroduced all the moral rot and spiritual corruption that had been scoured from the country when GOD dispossessed the pagan nations in favor of the children of Israel" (2 Kings 21:2). Manasseh allowed a sex-oriented religion to take over the amazing temple built in God's honor by Solomon in Jerusalem. Imagine how you'd feel if you arrived at school tomorrow and someone had taken over the gym and transformed it overnight into a holding pen for pigs. Or what would happen if you showed up at church only to discover that an adult bookstore had somehow bought the building and changed it into a sex and smut shopping mall? Then, as possibly the ultimate example of twisted religion, Manasseh joined others in sacrificing children to the gods as a form of worship. Sick!

You can be sure of one thing: God was not happy. Not only were his people treating his house with extreme disrespect, but they had clearly forgotten what God said would happen if they turned away from him once they got into the Promised Land. He had warned them disaster would fall. And one more important thing the people let slip: They forgot their history. They had loads of examples to prove that God always keeps his promises and his warnings. Long before the people fully realized it, God put them on the conveyor belt leading into the meat grinder of history.

After Manasseh died, his son Amon, a twenty-two-year-old, took the throne. He lasted two years. He basically dittoed everything his father had done. "He followed in the footsteps of his father, serving and worshiping the same foul gods his father had served. He totally deserted the GOD of his ancestors; he did not live GOD's way" (verses 21-22). Tired of Manasseh and Amon, the servants in the palace conspired and assassinated King Amon. That's how young Josiah came to be the new king.

Those were the wonder years—everyone wondered what kind of king Josiah would turn out to be. Would he be like his great grandfather Hezekiah, who all and all was a pretty good king? Or would he turn out to be like his grandfather and father and add his own chapter to the legacy of shameful behavior?

The first eight years of Josiah's reign give us no clues. But when he turned sixteen, he took a definite step in God's direction. The official record of his life that we find in 2 Chronicles says:

When he had been king for eight years — he was still only a teenager — he began to seek the God of David his ancestor. Four years later, the twelfth year of his reign, he set out to cleanse the neighborhood of sex-and-religion shrines, and get rid of the sacred Asherah groves and the god and goddess figurines, whether carved or cast, from Judah. He wrecked the Baal shrines, tore down the altars connected with them, and scattered the debris and ashes over the graves of those who had worshiped at them. He burned the bones of the priests on the same altars they had used when alive. He scrubbed the place clean, Judah and Jerusalem, clean inside and out. The cleanup campaign ranged outward to the cities of Manasseh, Ephraim, Simeon, and the surrounding neighborhoods — as far north as Naphtali. Throughout Israel he demolished the altars and Asherah

groves, pulverized the god and goddess figures, chopped up the neighborhood shrines into firewood. With Israel once more intact, he returned to Jerusalem. (34:3-7)

The king was young, but he carried a big stick, and over the next six years he used it to clean house. One minute it was a religious free-for-all where everything and anything was available, and the next Josiah blew the whistle on the huge corrupt mess. Some people probably said, "He's too young to know better. People aren't going to put up with him messing with their private lives and personal religion." They were partly right—he *was* too young to be drawn away by the evil that infested the land. When he made God the central person in his life, everything else fell into place.

Once Josiah returned to Jerusalem, he realized that it wasn't enough to try to wipe away all the filth and evil from the land; he had to do what he could to replace what had been bad with what was good. That's when he noticed the condition of Solomon's grand temple, which had been a symbol of God's special blessing on Israel. Yes, the idols and pagan shrines had been removed, but the place was in shambles. It looked like urban renewal before the renewal. The temple probably looked a little like your room after you've picked up all the dirty clothes and taken them to the laundry room. The place has improved, but not by that much!

It might not seem like a big deal, but Josiah learned a crucial lesson during that time, something that Jesus later described as the empty, clean space that welcomes an ever bigger mess (see Matthew 12:43-45). Whether it's bad habits, dirty laundry, or sinful behaviors, it's not enough to say, "Out with the old!" We have to also say, "In with the new!" If we've been reading stuff or looking at things online that have trashed our minds, it's not enough to stop doing that; we have to fill our minds with good stuff that will replace and displace the old bad stuff. This kind of internal renewal is what we read about in Romans 12:1-2:

> Take your everyday, ordinary life — your sleeping, eating, going-to-work, and walking-around life — and place it before God as an offering. Embracing what God does for you is the best thing you can do for him. Don't become so well-adjusted to your culture that you fit into it without even thinking. Instead, fix your attention on God. You'll be changed from the inside out. Readily recognize what he wants from you, and quickly respond to it. Unlike the culture around you, always dragging you down to its level of immaturity, God brings the best out of you, develops well-formed maturity in you.

Centuries before the New Testament was written, the spiritual principles that make life work were already in place. And Josiah was putting them into practice.

So the king arranged for a complete makeover. No, they didn't tear the temple down and rebuild it in like a week, and there wasn't a bus parked in front that had to be moved in order for the cleaned-up place to surprise everyone with the big "reveal." It was better than that. Lots of people got involved in the cleanup. And as often happens, under the trash, the workers found a treasure.

Here's where we meet another interesting character in our backstory. Today, we might call him Josiah's youth pastor. Hilkiah, the high priest, was the person in charge at the temple while the renovations were going on. In the rubble that had to be cleared away, the workers found an old scroll—a book. Think long piece of rolled-up leather with writing on it. When they unrolled the scroll, they found it was a copy of the fifth book of Moses—Deuteronomy. What a great discovery! And yet it also tells us that something was seriously wrong in that society: God's Word had been lost. Instead of God's daily guidance, it had become an archeological object or an antique. It had to be found in order to be read.

Hilkiah sent the scroll and a message to the king that God's book had been found. Imagine getting a note from your pastor that said, "Congratulations on your graduation. By the way, I just got an actual letter from God, and you're mentioned in it quite a few times. Wanna get together to read it?" That would at least pique your curiosity, right?

When Josiah heard what was in God's book, he was stunned. He probably felt a little like you would if you went for the yearly physical before school starts, and the doctor discovered in your tests that you had a terminal illness and only two weeks to live. So he sent you an official overnight letter of notification, but it got lost in the mail, and you didn't get the message until the day before you were supposed to die. Talk about bad news! You may not be sure what you would do in that situation, but Josiah got serious about making things right with God. He didn't waste any time.

He called for Hilkiah, Ahikam son of Shaphan, Abdon son of Micah, Shaphan the royal secretary, and Asaiah the king's personal aide. He ordered them all: "Go and pray to God for me and what's left of Israel and Judah. Find out what we must do in response to what is written in this book that has just been found! God's anger must be burning furiously against us — our ancestors haven't obeyed a thing written in this book of God, followed none of the instructions directed to us." (2 Chronicles 34:20–21)

So, you might be thinking, *what did Josiah hear that upset him so much*? Deuteronomy is Moses' summary of his career as the leader of the people of Israel, delivered shortly before he died. Right from the beginning, the book highlights the various ways God's chosen people treated God with resistance and rebellion. It makes it clear that the people spent forty years in the wilderness because they rejected God's guidance. Moses also reviewed the Ten Commandments God had given his people shortly after their departure from Egypt. But when Josiah got to chapter 17 of Deuteronomy, things got real personal for him:

When you enter the land that God, your God, is giving you and take it over and settle down, and then say, "I'm going to get me a king, a king like all the nations around me," make sure you get yourself a king whom God, your God, chooses. Choose your king from among your kinsmen; don't take a foreigner — only a kinsman. And make sure he doesn't build up a war machine, amassing military horses and chariots. He must not send people to Egypt to get more horses, because God told you, "You'll never go back there again!" And make sure he doesn't build up a harem, collecting wives who will divert him from the straight and narrow. And make sure he doesn't pile up a lot of silver and gold.

This is what must be done: When he sits down on the throne of his kingdom, the first thing he must do is make himself a copy of this Revelation on a
scroll, copied under the supervision of the Levitical priests. That scroll is to
remain at his side at all times; he is to study it every day so that he may learn
what it means to fear his God, living in reverent obedience before these rules
and regulations by following them. He must not become proud and arrogant,
changing the commands at whim to suit himself or making up his own versions.
If he reads and learns, he will have a long reign as king in Israel, he and his
sons. (verses 14–20)

Oops. Josiah was already eighteen years late on the "make himself a copy of this book" assignment. No wonder he tore his robe and humbled himself before God. He didn't make any excuses. He didn't waste any time with the lame "I didn't know" explanation. Instead, he consulted people he could trust: "We're in trouble. What do we do now?"

The word came back to Josiah from God: It's too late for the nation, but your humble and genuine response has bought everyone some time. Because you have kept God's Word as you knew it, you won't live to see the tragedy that falls on these people and this place (see 2 Chronicles 34:23-28).

Josiah did everything he could to bring his people back into right standing with God. Second Chronicles 35 describes his renewal of the yearly practice of the Passover, the celebration of God's orchestrated rescue of Israel from slavery in Egypt. He did it "by the book," like no one had done it for centuries. He set a tone of obedience for the nation he was leading. One summary of his life states,

> Josiah did a thorough job of cleaning up the pollution that had spread through-
> out Israelite territory and got everyone started fresh again, serving and
> worshiping their God. All through Josiah's life the people kept to the straight and
> narrow, obediently following God, the God of their ancestors. (2 Chronicles
> 34:33)

Congratulations! It's a Boy!

About the time Josiah was getting the nation back on track, Daniel and his friends were born. Several of them may have been babies present at the great Passover led by Josiah in the eighteenth year of his reign. For the next thirteen years, while they grew into young adulthood, Josiah led the people in a godly way and proved to be a hero. No doubt Daniel heard his parents say more than once, "Hope you grow up to be like Josiah." The fact that God's book had such a central impact on everything that Josiah did also affected the way Daniel and his friends were raised. They probably learned to read looking at copies of the scroll God had used to move the nation in the right direction. We don't know how widely it was known that God's message to Josiah had affirmed that God's judgment was still on its way, but even those who knew counted on some breathing room while Josiah remained king.

During your early years, whether or not you realized it, the people around you were pouring experience into your life. Mom and Dad and other family members have been telling stories, offering lessons, and living as examples of various kinds. You have been watching, hearing, and feeling all of this as it cascades into you. Some of it flowed through and some of it stuck. How much you benefit from your childhood experiences can't be immediately measured, but time will tell. In the case of Daniel and his friends, we may not know the specific details of their childhood, but based on how they lived later on, we can say with some confidence that those boys made excellent use of what they were offered as kids.

What about you?

Stressful Times
(Moves, New Places, Changes)

Change and stress almost always come hand in hand. As we've already said, even the best changes cause stress. It's just that the anticipated wonderful adventures of growing up have more subtle forms of stress. You may look forward to leaving home so much that you overlook all the details that will go into actually living on your own. Sometimes it's a rude awakening to realize that little background things like clean laundry, grocery shopping, and meals don't just happen automatically. Unless you've already learned to pick up after yourself, you may be puzzled to discover that everything pretty much stays right where you drop it until you decide to pick it up. And, needless to say, whatever you dropped is not going to wash itself and iron itself while it's lying there.

One of the troubling freedoms of living on your own is you discover that opening your food cabinet door is pretty much a waste of time if you haven't put anything in it earlier. The days of the magic refrigerator back home that always held delightful surprises and the basic food groups are over. You may be stuck with a single half-empty carton of milk that is emitting a suspicious odor . . . and a leftover sandwich spread with something that has turned green since you put it in there a few weeks ago. Meanwhile, your sock and underwear drawer is looking vacant, and you can't figure out why the clean replacements have been delayed. Might be time for a visit back home . . .

The point is that it's easy when you are growing up not to notice everything that's happening around you. It's easy to assume things get done almost by magic. Food gets cooked, rugs get vacuumed, dishes get washed . . . it's all a wonderful mystery when you think of it. One of the reasons it's such a hassle to be asked to take out the garbage or fill the dishwasher is that deep down you think, *Why do I have to do this when all it takes is magic?*

Even if you have a job when you are young, you are not usually expected to turn that money over to pay for your living expenses at home. Income from a part-time job is considered play money that you get to spend on whatever you wish. Living on your own can put a serious dent in the play money account. It comes as quite a shock when you suddenly realize how much everything costs when you have to come up with the cash on your own! The transition from living in an all-expenses-paid childhood home to a you're-on-your-own lifestyle can be an awakening. And it often comes with a share of stress.

Dose of Reality

When we last saw our young heroes, they were growing up under the kingly rule of Josiah, enjoying life in Jerusalem. There might have been trouble brewing in the world teapot, but things close to home were pretty stable. Those in the know, like the parents of Dan and his friends, must have had a sense that their children would end up dealing with God's judgment on the nation after Josiah was gone. But there wasn't much they could do except focus on the task at hand, bringing up kids who had an awareness of God and knew he was ultimately in control of the world.

Then word reached Jerusalem that the army of Egypt was on the move, marching up the coast on the west side of Israel, headed to war with the Babylonians. For reasons that still remain unclear, Josiah decided he would engage the Egyptians in battle. This is like the smallest dog on the block deciding to nip at the largest canine in the territory, an animal the neighbors suspect might be a wolf in disguise. Neco, the king of Egypt, tried to convince Josiah that he was stepping into a situation that wasn't his business. There's no indication that Josiah asked God about the wisdom of what he was doing, one of the few missteps in the king's life.

Josiah also decided he would go into battle undercover. He put on a disguise as a common soldier and took to the field. The Egyptian archers, firing arrows toward Israel's forces, unintentionally wounded Josiah. He asked his secret service guys to get him out of there, so they put him in an ambulance chariot and took him back to Jerusalem. Shortly thereafter, he died. What a sad, unnecessary loss. The great prophet Jeremiah showed up for the funeral and composed an "anthem of lament" to honor the king. Josiah was only thirty-nine when he died.

If you've read his story in the Bible, you might be wondering, *What about God's promise in 2 Chronicles 34:28 — "I'll take care of you; you'll have a quiet death and be buried in peace. You won't be around to see the doom that I'm going to bring upon this place and people"? Did God lose track of Josiah?* That's a good question. The first point we need to make is that God doesn't give us promises to encourage us to do stupid stuff. That was a little trick the devil tried with Jesus when he suggested that it would be fine for Jesus to jump off a roof because God had promised to protect him. Jesus knew that would be a bad move, and he rejected the devil's suggestion. That same devil may have whispered in Josiah's ear, "Hey, you've got God's protection; go for it!"

It's also worth noting that Josiah didn't die in battle, despite his unwise actions. He died back in Jerusalem, in his own bed. None of this caught God by surprise. He was managing things on the big stage of history, and he was also handling things with his chosen people.

Youthful Grief

The death of a childhood hero hits hard. Daniel and his friends were probably at the state funeral for King Josiah. The first person close to you who dies — grandparent, parent, friend, or hero—leaves a powerful impression on your view of life. For many, it's the first time they think they hear death whisper to them, "I'm waiting for you, too." The thought can scare you, but it can also make you look at life with a new sense of appreciation.

Josiah's death brought some quick changes in Daniel's life. Josiah's son Jehoahaz ascended to the throne by popular demand. We don't know why, but his time as king lasted only three months. The king of Egypt began to exert control over Judah. Under Neco's threats, Jerusalem had to pay a huge sum to prevent an attack. Neco also took it upon himself to replace Jehoahaz with one of Josiah's other sons, whom he named Jehoiakim. Twenty-five years old when he became king, Jehoiakim ruled for eleven years. In that time, he did his best to undo much of the good his father had accomplished. But his sponsor, Neco, was defeated by the rising Babylonians, and Jehoiakim had to deal with almost constant harassment from invaders.

To make things worse, Jehoiakim decided he didn't want to pay protection money to the Babylonians any longer. Three years after he became king, in 605 BC, Jehoiakim revolted and Nebuchadnezzar's forces slapped him down. The Babylonian army passed through Judah and took whatever they wanted. Among the items ordered by Nebuchadnezzar was a hand-picked group of bright, young Jews who were to be removed from their families and from Jerusalem and shipped off to Babylon. Or to put it in official language: "The king told Ashpenaz, head of the palace staff, to get some Israelites from the royal family and nobility—young men who were healthy and handsome, intelligent and well-educated, good prospects for leadership positions in the government, perfect specimens!" (Daniel 1:3-4). As near as we can tell, Daniel and his friends were probably sixteen or seventeen years old at the time.

The selection committee headed up by Ashpenaz began to interview people in Jerusalem to find the best candidates for his one-way foreign exchange program. He was subtle about his purpose. What would happen if someone showed up at your school and announced at an all-school assembly, "I'm evaluating all of you in the process of identifying a small, select few who will be shipped off on a difficult journey to a faraway place and you will never see your families again—so impress me with your abilities and academic prowess!" You can imagine the results of that news. When that assembly was dismissed, the crowd would have suddenly become a herd of bumbling idiots! This was not the all-expenses-paid scholarship anyone was looking for.

So the Babylonians were stealthy. They asked around: Who are the young people from royal families who have already made a mark for themselves in school and in society? Who has been voted most eligible to succeed? Who are the leaders in this school? We don't know how many were chosen, but clearly Daniel, Hananiah, Mishael, and Azariah were at the top of the list.

The summer of 605 BC had Jerusalem in a panic. No sooner had Jehoiakim let it be known that Judah would no longer be sending shipments of gold and silver to Babylon, the army of Nebuchadnezzar came knocking. Shocked by the quick and overwhelming response, the king didn't put up a fight. He opened the city to the Babylonians. They immediately confiscated some of the precious items that were part of the temple property—things that had been dedicated for use in honor of God. These were boxed up and sent to Babylon via UPS (Ur Parcel Service). As bad as that was, the next development was a blow to the heart of several families.

One evening, Daniel was having dinner with his family on the terrace at home, talking about what might happen in the next few years. So far, the Babylonians seemed content to take the items from the temple and leave people alone. The food supply hadn't been disrupted too badly by the invading army, so folks still had plenty to eat. Daniel's parents hoped that by cooperating with the Babylonians, the city might be spared the kind of fate they had heard about regarding other cities.

Daniel and his friends had noticed that strangers had been around, taking notes the last few days, but foreigners were always coming and going in Jerusalem, so it hadn't seemed that unusual. Only when they looked over the city walls and saw the city of tents, the drilling soldiers, and the packed chariot parking lots had they sensed some concern about the future.

The meal was interrupted by a firm pounding on the door to the street. A servant answered and then came to inform Daniel and his father that they were being requested at the gate. Puzzled, they hurried across the courtyard and approached the open door. The street was crowded with soldiers in unfamiliar uniforms. But among them Daniel immediately saw the worried faces of his three friends and other young people. Without a word, the commanding soldier stepped forward, placed his hand on Daniel's shoulder, looked at his father, and said, "This young man has been chosen for the grand privilege of serving in the court of the great King Nebuchadnezzar. We leave for Babylon immediately." He firmly pulled Daniel through the doorway before his father could do or say anything, and the entire group began to move quickly up the street. Daniel hadn't realized his mother had followed them from the terrace, but the last thing he heard from his family were the anguished cries of his mother and the murmured words of his father as he tried in vain to comfort his wife.

It's one thing to send applications to a college or university and get offers or gentle rejections in response. You can look online and take virtual tours of campuses, weighing all the benefits and liabilities of distance and reputation as you decide which school you will attend. But you wouldn't expect one of the universities to send a squad of campus police to your house to immediately escort you to your new life away from home at school. The transition from living at home to moving away usually happens gradually, and there are frequent returns for special occasions. The idea of being taken away suddenly, without so much as a toothbrush, would leave most of us stunned and confused.

Stress is a relative thing, and most of us are not going to experience the kind of stress that Daniel went through. The takeaway from his experience is to remember that people have gone through much worse than we're dealing with, and with

God's help, they made it. Wouldn't it make sense to expect God to help us make it through whatever stress we have to face?

Daniel and his friends were in good health, but they hadn't expected to spend their summer on a five-hundred-mile hike north from Jerusalem and then southeast along the Euphrates River to Babylon. They were actually reversing the travels of the father of the Jewish nation, Abraham, who had followed God's guidance going the opposite way, in order to arrive at the Promised Land.

The boys were forced to move at army pace, covering miles on foot each day. Their break from the environment where they had spent their childhood was devastatingly complete. They had little time to wonder what waited for them in Babylon. They spent each day trying to keep up. Covering ten to fifteen miles a day on foot means it took them almost two grueling months to reach Babylon.

Foot-Dragging

While the boys from Jerusalem are dragging their feet along the length of the Fertile Crescent, let's consider some possible foot-dragging of your own. You probably have the luxury of knowing when you will be leaving home. For example, when Matt turned thirteen, his father had a memorable conversation with him:

Dad: "So, you've reached thirteen, the start of seven years as a teen."

Matt: "Yeah, Dad."

Dad: "Actually, I want to talk about the next *five* years, up to when you turn eighteen."

Matt: "Hmmm. Eighteen."

Dad: "I know five years sounds like a long time, but believe me it's going to go quick. What it means to your mom and me is that we can count on five more years of you being a regular part of our household. Then you'll be leaving."

Matt hadn't really thought about it that way before. It almost felt like his father was telling him he would *have* to leave at eighteen. He kind of mumbled, "Are you guys kicking me out when I turn eighteen?"

Dad: "We wouldn't put it that way. We just know that you'll be done with high school and ready to move on by then. It's not that we *want* you to go, but we want to be ready so that your leaving is a good experience for all of us. So, what do you want to do between now and then with your family?"

They talked about some trips and other activities that the family enjoyed, and Matt expressed his interest in experiencing those things during the years he had left at home. They came up with a plan. When Matt eventually left home at eighteen, it wasn't easy, but both he and his family remember that as a special time because they faced it together and were enthusiastic about sending their grown-up member out into the world.

As the reality of departure time settles in, it's normal for some foot-dragging to kick in. You may feel like the young bird that couldn't wait to fly but now is a little worried as its mother gently pushes it farther and farther toward the end of the branch.

Its little brain is thinking, *I'm looking forward to flying; I'm not liking looking down or the fact that before I can fly, I'll have to drop.*

When takeoff time approaches, "last" experiences take on added significance:

- Last time you mow the lawn
- Final locker clean-out at school
- Final time you sit together in church as a family
- Last time going out as a family to your favorite restaurant

It's not that you will never participate in these activities or visit these places again, but this is the last time you participate for a while. The next time, if it comes, you'll be another one of the adults in the picture. At some point, you may even get to pick up the check.

Disorientation

Even under the best of circumstances, like when your parents pack you up and drive you to college, the moments following separation can have a powerful disorienting effect. It's not so much the distance (whether you go to school across town or across the country) but the sense of space between you. You are no longer under the same roof. Even in the age of cell phones, Skype, and easy travel, when you leave home you are suddenly aware that others who mean something to you are not as *available.* Yes, you can still talk, but it's going to take more effort, a decision on your part.

You may have gotten used to (and probably a little irritated over) Mom or Dad's habit of asking twenty questions every time you walked in the door. Now you come back to your dorm room or apartment, and no one is there to check in with. No one cares how your day went. Nobody asks questions, even ones you're not eager to answer. In order to get your "care and irritation" fix, you will have to contact home. If you're wise, you'll realize it's worth making the effort. It's important to stay in touch. One of the best stress-busters is the mature decision to contact people who love you and let them know you're okay. They almost come with a guarantee of concern for you that can make a huge difference when you are faced with a daily sense that you are surrounded by a world that couldn't care less.

Dead Zones Before Cell Phones

For Daniel and his friends, there would be no phoning home. Not only couldn't they get any "bars" where they were, they had to leave their cell phones behind. Years would pass before there was any news from their families. But such a complete break with their past also had the effect of cementing their relationship with each other. Whatever lay ahead, they were in this together, and they knew that God was with them as much on the road to Babylon as he had been back at home in Jerusalem.

So expect some disorientation. You will feel out of balance. Of course, this varies with each person. It can be a wise move to call home or reach out to a friend "from the old days" and see how he or she is doing. Take some time to look into the lives of other young people in the Bible who left home, like Ruth, Esther, John, Mark, and Timothy. In particular, look for the signs of disorientation when they left home and how they dealt with the experience. Note how important in each of their lives was the presence of an older mentor who guided them through the transition. People like Naomi, Mordecai, Barnabas, and Paul can have a balancing effect on you. As with these biblical examples, some were from their past and some were from their present, but the relationship steadied the young person. You may want to set up a weekly call with your small-group leader from home, join a Christian group on campus and meet with the leader, or contact a student leader from your youth group who is an upperclassman at college. You can also ask a trusted adult in your life to recommend a Christian mentor. Finding someone like this will add stability as you orient yourself to your new situation.

Also remember that life is about change, but God never changes. Life will take you places, but God will already be there when you arrive, and He never leaves you while you are on your way. There's an important sense in which moving away gives you the chance to respond to some of God's direction in a new and different way than when you were growing up. Up until this point, your life has always been in the context of your family, and your parents had an immediate say on the choices you made. That's changing. You are about to face opportunities like those Jesus described in his final words to his disciples—not as a kid anymore but as an adult who can make decisions and take action. Jesus said,

> Go out and train everyone you meet, far and near, in this way of life, marking them by baptism in the threefold name: Father, Son, and Holy Spirit. Then instruct them in the practice of all I have commanded you. I'll be with you as you do this, day after day after day, right up to the end of the age. (Matthew 28:19-20)

The lines of obedience are more direct now. Up to this point, you've followed Jesus as a member of your family. But from now on, your opportunities to respond to Jesus' guidance will be more immediate. You are his representative in your new world. And given what Jesus said above, the most immediate issue you need to decide is, do you know "this way of life" well enough to pass it on to others? In what ways can you begin to use your life and practices as examples when you "instruct" others about what it means to be a Christian? Like we've said, being on your own brings both the freedom and responsibility to live as Christ wants you to live.

Stressful times are also indications that you're alive. You're not a rock; you're a human organism, designed to function in miraculous ways every single day. The sensitivities to the environment around you that we call "stress" are part of the unique design God gave you. Count on him to help you make the best use of those signals. Sometimes stress tells you to slow down (or speed up). It may be a sign to stop. It may be an early warning that you're going the wrong way and need to turn around.

Or it may just be the way you are adjusting to a new adventure and opportunity in life that God has placed before you for your good and to benefit other people.

A Rough Landing
(Old Life and New Culture)

Your first weeks away from home are going to be a critical adjustment period for you. Settling into a new place, even if it's a school dorm room, is actually an opportunity to discover and express a lot of truth about yourself. As the old saying somewhat goes, you can take the kid out of the messy room but you can't necessarily take the messy room out of the kid! If you are not intentional about what you want to change (and what you want to keep the same) in your new location, soon it will tend to look like your old location.

Think about what you are going to take with you. You may be tempted to take *everything* from your old life, but moving out of the house can be a wonderful chance to simplify your possessions. Talk to your parents and discuss the expectations you and they have for your room and your things. They may be hoping to use your room for something else, or they might want you to keep things there that make you feel at home when you return for holidays and breaks. Once you've determined what the plan is for your room, you'll have a much better idea of what you need to do with your possessions, what to keep, what to toss, and what to take with you to school.

You will be amazed how much clutter you have accumulated in less than twenty years of life. Make three piles (or three lists in case the piles get too big). Pile One will be stuff to take. Pile Two will be stuff to get rid of—keeping everything you have written, drawn, or scribbled since you were in first grade is probably overkill and maybe a little OCD. But your parents (and later on your own kids) may get a kick out of some of your report cards and samples of your "early" work. Pile Three will be stuff you want to keep but can't take with you right now so you hope your parents will be willing to store for you. If your parents see that you are making the effort to cull your stuff, they will be much more understanding and open to the idea of holding some things temporarily for you. Remember, if you're coming home for the summers and your parents say it's okay to leave some things in your room, you might go through this process a few times. Getting some distance from your things will give you more clarity on what you really need to save. Don't overwhelm yourself trying to make hundreds of decisions the first time around.

Unless someone really insists that you "leave your room exactly the way it was when you lived here," don't. Pack up the possessions you aren't taking and label the boxes for your own benefit later. Four or five years from now, you won't remember what you put in the banana box and what was in the vintage wine carton. Once you've secured permission to store the boxes in the attic or garage, move them there yourself. If parents and siblings want to help you, that's great, but you will go a long way in demonstrating that you are ready to live on your own if you take responsibility for your stuff. Making all these decisions will be stressful, but good for you. It's what grown-ups do.

Back to Pile One—the stuff you decide to take with you. Before you stack it and pack it, take a breath. Practice the "deserted island" routine. If you were going to be marooned at sea with the stuff you're taking, how much of it would you actually use? Suddenly, the snowmobile doesn't seem like that great an item, right? Unless you're renting a large U-Haul truck and have unlimited space, you may not be able to take everything you'd eventually like to have with you. Think about the space at the other end. Your roommate in the dorm may not be all that excited if, after you've moved in all your stuff, he or she is left with about two square feet of space to call their own. Leave most of your summer clothes behind (unless you're headed for Sahara Polytechnic—in which case you can leave most of the winter gear at home). So, some stuff from Pile One will end up in Pile Three at least temporarily.

You may be hyperventilating as you read this stuff about packing—that's stress rearing its ugly head. But you're going to have to face the pressure of packing head-on. Believe us, it's *more* stressful to put it off. The best way to deal with the stress of organizing for a move is to have a plan. If you don't have a system, the stress will eat you alive. The only way to avoid the stress of packing is to leave everything behind (and face a different kind of stress). That's what happened with Dan and company.

Departure

Let's get back to our stress heroes in Israel. When the soldiers collected the young people designated for deportation to Babylon, there was no time for sorting, packing, or even saying proper good-byes. They apparently left with little but the shirts on their backs.

Dan and his friends arrived in Babylon late in the summer of 605 BC, just in time for the first day of classes at Babel On U. They were tanned, toughened, and tired. Two months of Babylonian military MRE (Meal, Ready-to-Eat) rations had left them a little on the light side but probably in the best shape of their lives. Who knows what kind of infections, diseases, and other life dangers they survived on their trek from Jerusalem. The fact that they never wrote about these things doesn't mean they didn't go through them.

As they walked the streets of the Babylonian capital, their heads swiveled constantly and their senses were overwhelmed. Many of the sights, smells, and sounds were new to them. They were impressed by the magnificent gardens and modern buildings; they were now in a city that made the list as one of the seven wonders of the world. They were proud of Jerusalem as the city of David, but they were awed by the excesses and beauties of the new empire that Nebuchadnezzar's father had passed on to his son. These were structures and temples like they had never seen before.

At the street level things were very different than Dan and his friends were used to back home. Unusual people from the far-flung corners of the world flocked (or were brought in chains) to Babylon, and they created quite a kaleidoscope of races and costumes. The boys themselves were the constant objects of discussions and questions. They were thankful their schooling back in Jerusalem had included fluency in the Aramaic language, which was the trade and court language of Babylon. They made an immediate impression on the curious when they understood what was being said to them (and about them) and answered clearly in the official language. Not having to take the remedial Aramaic language class their first year of college immediately put them in an advanced group of scholars.

As official foreign exchange students sponsored by the court, Dan and his friends were not allowed to determine their course of study. King Nebuchadnezzar had decided what their advanced degrees were going to be: "Babylonian language and the lore of magic and fortunetelling" (Daniel 1:4). That sounds a little like studying the original version of the Harry Potter stories. In other words, these Jewish boys were going to have to master subjects that their families considered forbidden.

Colleges do have a way of imposing certain classes on you. Some of this involves graduation requirements. You're expected to know how to read and write intelligently by the time you leave school. If you manage to get through four years of under-graduate education and remain illiterate, it looks bad for the school. So they often have a list of must-take courses that you have to endure. Some of these courses will expose you to ideas you might not have pursued if you were only taking subjects that interested you. If you are going to a Christian college or university, expect to be required to take a certain number of Bible and related courses, regardless of the field your degree represents. In a parallel way, if you are going to a secular school, realize that you will have to take some courses that could be described as "secular religion." You may find the Christian faith ridiculed or dismissed in these classes, and you may feel ineffective in presenting your side of things because the "deck is stacked against you."

No doubt Daniel and his friends went through the same difficulties (more on this later). To the Babylonians, the God of Israel might have seemed pretty weak, since he failed to protect his people from the invader. Daniel wasn't in a position to say or do much at that point, but he left things in God's hands and kept his attention focused on the immediate challenges.

Interestingly enough, the schooling they were about to enter was scheduled to take three years. Apparently the Babylonians thought that was enough time to train someone to function in some capacity in the court. Daniel and his friends were being trained to be government workers, though their excellent record and eventual performance moved them quickly to the head of the class. We can compare their experience with the length of a campus experience you will have in a standard program at the undergraduate level. There's no indication that they had summers off or long spring breaks for trips to Fort Lauderdale. So their three years of continual schooling probably equaled at least four years of today's schedule.

New ID

Before they decided what to do about their education, Daniel and his friends got another unexpected surprise. When they registered for school, they discovered someone had stolen their identities. This wasn't an Internet scam. The king's servant Ashpenaz informed them that they were being assigned new names—Babylonian names. To us, the names Daniel, Hananiah, Mishael, and Azariah are anything but familiar, but as in many cultures, the names parents gave their children in Israel were actually phrases that meant something. We can see a similar pattern in English when it comes to people's last names: Miller, Shoemaker, Smith, and Wright are all names that used to be primarily occupations. So Joseph, the town miller, eventually became Joseph Miller. And Alexander, who was a smith specializing in copper work, eventually became Alexander Coppersmith.

Well, Jewish names followed that pattern, but the themes of the names were about God, not jobs. As a result, Daniel means, "God is my judge." Each time someone called this young man's name, they were also recognizing something about themselves and God. A king like Nebuchadnezzar would not have been pleased to have to admit "God is my judge" every time he said Daniel's name. So Ashpenaz issued new names to the four star students: Daniel became Belteshazzar ("he whom Bel"—one of the Babylonian gods—"favors"); Hananiah, whose name meant "Jehovah God has been merciful," became Shadrach ("under the command of Aku"—another Babylonian god); Mishael, "who is like God," became Meshach ("who is like Aku"); and Azariah, "Jehovah has helped," became Abednego ("one who serves Nebo"—the fire god). Fortunately for us, Daniel kept his name throughout most of the book that tells his life. His three friends, however, are better known by their Babylonian names than their Hebrew ones.

What's in a Name?

Now that you are leaving home, you're going to entrust your name to a lot of new people. Your name is a chunk of your identity. When people remember it, you may feel good about that because they remembered you. But you have also given them the ability to get your attention. It's hard not to respond when someone calls your name. Telling people our name involves a certain amount of risk, because they may misuse it. At the same time, exchanging names is one of the first steps toward friendship. If we can't trust each other with our names, we probably can't be friends.

The point here is not to make you hesitate to tell others your name. Just the opposite is the case. How you handle the names of others can make a definite impression. If you make an effort to remember someone's name, it shows that you value them. If they have to keep introducing themselves to you, they will feel you don't care enough to recall their name.

When you are moving into a college situation where you will be deluged with new names, being intentional about remembering certain people's names may not seem like a big deal, but it will mean a lot to others. This may not be a skill that comes naturally to you. Believe us, it's not easy for a lot of people. You may want to make a little chart of the rooms around you and label it with the names. Connecting memorable features with the names can be one trick to help you remember—Joe the only redhead on your floor, Pete with the gray streaks in his first beard, Tim with the great laugh. Choose positive features and you'll find yourself saying the names in a friendly way.

Handling the Rough Landing

When you arrive at school, you will feel disoriented. Maybe that's why they have these gatherings called Freshman Orientation—to repair your disorientation. And you may feel like you're a klutz who's unable to figure out simple things that everyone around you already seems to know. But do the math: At least 25 percent of the people around you are also freshmen and new students who don't have a clue. Figure some of them are just doing a good job of pretending. Give yourself (depending on your terminology) at least three free passes, mulligans, or do-overs each day. That means you can get lost three times, or have to ask directions three times, or forget where you're supposed to be three times each day in the first week without stressing over it. You know you're going around a learning curve, so there's going to be some pressure, but you'll get through this bend in the road of life and hit the straightaway soon.

Before you arrive at the campus, file a flight plan for yourself. Do as much of the registering, class choosing, and those kinds of decisions ahead of time. Lots of your freshman courses will be boilerplate requirements, and choosing certain instructors probably won't be a big factor. As you move through school, those choices will become more and more important. Instructors often make the class. Make it a habit to get a reference from a current student when you're planning to take a course or instructor the next semester. What you can calmly prepare for will cut way down on the stress load you have to carry.

Dan and his friends took the required courses, but they kept their heads and hearts in tune with the truth. They didn't automatically accept the widely held idea that college is all about abandoning everything you've learned in order to choose your own new set of beliefs and values (which turns out to be a set of pretty narrow and predictable values that fit the world's patterns). You may, and should, learn a lot. But you are not required, nor is it necessarily wise, to give up what you've already learned. Just because you now have to really think for yourself doesn't mean that what you've been told at home or growing up is all wrong. If someone tells you that, pay careful attention to what he or she is trying to sell you as a replacement!

Realize that much like Daniel and his friends experienced, your relationship with God will be under assault when you first move away. You have to operate on your own, perhaps for the first time in your life, so you may be seen as an easy target, not only by other people but by Satan himself. He would like nothing better than to get a young Christian doubting, confused, and convinced to turn their back on the central relationship in their lives. If that happens, the landing will just keep getting worse. Make it your goal to preserve your daily relationship with God, and you will find yourself more easily able to handle what's ahead for you. Visit local churches until you find one grounded in the Bible where you can get involved and grow your relationship with Christ and other believers. Just as Daniel had his three friends in the faith, by maintaining your routine of going to church and finding support with other believers, you too can survive these stressful times.

4

Buffet or à la Carte?
(Stress-Based or Wisdom-Based Choices)

Ian was not a large young man, but he made somewhat of a reputation for himself on his college campus as the LAP (Largest Appetite per Pound) champion. He and a couple of friends sealed their "big bite" status among their peers when they were officially banned from the downtown smorgasbord in Greenville, Illinois. They showed up for the all-you-can-eat special on Sunday afternoon and didn't stop eating until they were begged to leave. They politely told the owner that he ought to consider the vast quantities of food they had consumed as a compliment to his chef. He told them he couldn't afford those kinds of compliments. Imagine for a moment having your picture on a Not Wanted poster in a restaurant! Ian was never one to go to an à la carte establishment if there was a buffet within driving distance. *À la carte,* in case your high school French has failed you, means that you order from the menu.

Buffet (another tasty French word) means, basically, you can eat anything in sight!

Graduating and moving away from home will push you into having to take more responsibility for your life. You're bound to make some mistakes and do some silly and even foolish things along the way. Ask older people what they remember most about college, and one of the points they usually bring up involves all the things they wish they could forget. The objective of life lessons is to teach us wisdom. We learn wisdom primarily from three sources: our own experiences, observing the experiences of others (what we see and what they tell us), and listening to God. The fact is, the more we pay attention to sources one and two and then compare what we learn to source three, the more we realize that the most reliable place to find wisdom is in God's Word. Our experiences and the wisdom of others at best simply confirm the truth of God's Word. As Eugene Peterson, the translator of *The Message*, puts it,

> "Wisdom" is the biblical term for this on-earth-as-it-is-in-heaven everyday living. Wisdom is the art of living skillfully in whatever actual conditions we find ourselves. It has virtually nothing to do with information as such, with knowledge as such. . . .
>
> Wisdom has to do with becoming skillful in honoring our parents and raising our children, handling our money and conducting our sexual lives, going to work and exercising leadership, using words well and treating friends kindly, eating and drinking healthily, cultivating emotions within ourselves and attitudes toward others that make for peace. Threaded through all these items is

the insistence that the way we think of and respond to God is the most practical thing we do. . . .

In matters of everyday practicality, nothing, absolutely nothing, takes precedence over God.[1]

Peterson was writing about the Bible in general and about the book of Proverbs in particular. This collection of wise sayings would have been familiar to Dan and his friends. The book of Daniel reports that the boys were identified by Ashpenaz as people who exhibited a lot of wisdom. That means they were practicing what God's Word had to say about living. We have every reason to believe that as a result of the reforms King Josiah put in place before his death, Dan and his friends had a chance to grow up in an atmosphere where God's Word was respected. The fact that recent kings had gone off on their own and rebelled against God didn't mean the message of the Old Testament books had no affect on the lives of these young men. After all, Jeremiah the prophet was very active in Jerusalem in the years leading up to the deportation of the boys. They may have had direct contact with him. Since we know how the boys lived when they were on their own, we can see that they were influenced by the godly people around them rather than the people who, along with King Jehoiakim, wanted to live outside God's direction.

Babel On U Student Union

Daniel and his friends were still growing boys. They certainly didn't mind getting called to dinner. There they were, far from home cooking and life as they had known it, yet they were being given special treatment. In a sense, they had been kidnapped from their homeland and were now being managed in a new land by people who wanted to gain their loyalty. As a way of building their trust, King Nebuchadnezzar directed that their menu would be the same as his. Whatever his personal chef prepared, the quantity had to be large enough to feed the star pupils from Israel. They were issued platinum meal plan cards. They didn't have to go through the cafeteria food line at the student union; their meals were brought to the executive dining hall and served on expensive china. The book of Daniel describes the arrangement: "The king then ordered that they be served from the same menu as the royal table—the best food, the finest wine. After three years of training they would be given positions in the king's court" (Daniel 1:5).

Preemptive Decisions

Daniel understood one of the important lessons about living a healthy life; he learned to make decisions *before* they had to be made. The more significant the issue, the more crucial it becomes to think through the decision ahead of time so that when the choice presents itself, the answer is a no-brainer.

Too many people live with shoot-from-the-hip decision-making. They put off thinking about the details and consequences of choices until the last moment. They avoid making decisions until they must. But that's when the pressure of the situation and the lack of preparation lead to impulsive choices that people have to live with for years—sometimes forever. How we feel in the moment is the poorest reason to make a certain decision. Choosing a milk shake flavor is a decision you can make in the moment, but deciding what kind of person you will marry or how you will respond to certain situations, like the opportunity to cheat, should never be put off to the last moment. These are decisions to make before they have to be made!

In the account of Daniel's arrival in Babylon, a note is included about one such "ahead of time" decision this young man made: "But Daniel determined that he would not defile himself by eating the king's food or drinking his wine, so he asked the head of the palace staff to exempt him from the royal diet" (verse 8). Daniel wasn't waiting until situations came up; he was creating certain patterns in his life that he wanted to follow no matter what opportunities came his way. In this case, the decision on Daniel's part was, "I'm not going to defile myself." Daniel made a profound choice about life long before the king's food and wine were offered to him. Saying "no thanks" to the king's menu wasn't hard because Daniel had already made the hard decision not to defile himself.

You may well be asking, "What was Daniel thinking? What does it mean to defile oneself?" Good question. Defiling has to do with compromising, ruining, and betraying. It means using something that was intended for one purpose and twisting it for use in a different and opposite purpose. An obvious example of defilement in today's world would be pumping water into your car's gas tank—the vehicle has been defiled.

But you probably wouldn't use the term "defiled" to describe the results. You'd say, "What vehicle? That's now a pile of rusting metal!" On a more personal level, deceiving a friend would be a painful example of defiling a relationship. Or in a more intimate area, if you grow up knowing that saving the sexual side of yourself for marriage would be a precious and unique gift you could present to the person with whom you are going to spend your life, but you put yourself in situations where you make other decisions about sex "in the heat of the moment." The precious gift has been defiled. It can still be given, but it won't be the same. The point is that defilement is a big deal. Something valuable is ruined or lost when it is defiled. Choosing not to defile what we have and who we are almost always causes stress in day-to-day living, but that pressure doesn't compare to the stress and sorrow of realizing that what we once thought of as very valuable is now defiled.

By deciding not to defile himself, Daniel was drawing a mark in the sand of life and saying, "Here's one line I'm not going to cross." He understood that there are places we shouldn't go, people we shouldn't be with, things we shouldn't do — not necessarily because those things are bad in themselves, but because our connection with them will affect how we are seen and may well injure our relationship with God. Food really wasn't the central issue here. Daniel was preserving his own integrity. He was keeping his word, even when it was a promise he had made to himself!

The most intimate understanding of defilement does have to do with our relationship with God. We recognize that God calls us to be holy, which means taking his creation and ownership of us seriously. Ultimately, the deepest promises we make are between ourselves and God. This is why, for instance, when we speak the vows (promises) of marriage, we acknowledge that we are saying them before witnesses who include God himself. These promises are as serious as life itself. Promises, once they are made, can only be kept or broken — they can't be "unmade." If promises can be changed or rejected on a whim, they don't mean much. But most of us *do* want our promises to be worth something to others. We *want* people to be able to count on our word — all the more when it comes to God. We put ourselves in real danger if we make promises to God that we don't intend to keep. And the promises we make to God will probably cost us something to keep. When Daniel determined to avoid defilement, he couldn't know what specific challenges that decision would bring, but he made the decision and kept it.

The king's food probably looked good and smelled delicious — and it may have even tasted better! That wasn't the issue. And if Daniel had been trying to make decisions about life on the fly, he would have had a harder time turning away. Most of us think that if it looks good, smells wonderful, and promises to taste good — we should probably eat it! But there's also an interesting warning in Proverbs:

> Don't accept a meal from a tightwad;
>> don't expect anything special.
> He'll be as stingy with you as he is with himself;
>> he'll say, "Eat! Drink!" but won't mean a word
>>> of it.

His miserly serving will turn your stomach
when you realize the meal's a sham.
   (Proverbs 23:6–8)

The practical warning involves the principle of "strings attached." Accepting a gift can put you in someone's debt—like someone who claims to be your friend, but then you discover he wants you to back him up when he is doing or saying something wrong. The cost of that friendship involves you in an activity (like lying) that you don't want to do. Yes, friends stick together through good times and hard times, but friends don't ask friends to defile themselves. And gifts that require "payback" aren't really gifts.

Daniel knew that giving in on "little things" would make it very difficult to stand firm on harder things later on. He was right. When a "friend" asks you to supply "a little help on my homework by letting me copy yours," you can be sure it isn't going to stop there. But once you start along that path, how do you stop? It's one thing to help a friend; it's another to have a friend think it's okay for you to defile yourself.

It's hard to get through high school without discovering from experience that "friends" covers a large group of people, but not all friendships are equal. There may be some sense of accomplishment when we can point to hundreds of "friends" on an Internet site, but the truth is, the word *friend* is now so overused that it can rarely stand alone. Instead we have BFFs. By the time most of us walk across the stage at graduation, what we know is that the best as well as the most painful experiences we've had so far in life have all involved people we called "friends."

When it came to their relationship with King Nebuchadnezzar, Daniel and his friends made it clear from the start that they accepted their situation as captured servants of the king but would not allow it to undermine their ultimate allegiance to God. So the king's table was off limits. History tells us that among the frequent menu items in the king's cafeteria would have been pork, which was a forbidden meat for Jews. Based on that nonkosher factor, the boys from Israel would have been uncomfortable even hanging out at the king's salad bar—bacon bits and all. This was a point of integrity and faithfulness. But the next step is what makes this a great example of wisdom as well as an excellent lesson in how to deal with stressful situations.

The Creative Alternative

There are some opportunities in life that simply require a "no" response. Others can best be handled with a "how about this instead?" Sometimes we feel so much pressure when we know we have to reject a request that we miss the wise tactic of the creative alternative. We mentioned in the last section the instance of a friend who approaches us to ask for our answers on a test. We don't want to be accessories to a wrong action, but we also feel the importance of helping a friend. What we need to realize is that we don't have to let that person define what the help will be. We can gently say "no" to the cheating while saying "yes" to helping them figure out their own answers. This not only keeps the issues clear, but it allows us to discover what kind of friendship this really is—if someone insists that we prove our friendship by helping them do something wrong, that person is already demonstrating they are not our friend.

Dan and his friends were at the bottom of several levels of supervision. At the top of the pile was King Nebuchadnezzar. Next came Ashpenaz, the king's right-hand man regarding the personnel in the palace. He was the palace HR professional. He assigned one of his assistants to be a valet or overseer of the training of this particular class of foreign captives. Once Dan realized there was a potential problem with the king's meal plan, the strategy he took is one of the best examples we have in the Bible of the wise and creative alternative. Daniel arranged for an appointment with Ashpenaz and talked about the situation:

> Daniel determined that he would not defile himself by eating the king's food or drinking his wine, so he asked the head of the palace staff to exempt him from the royal diet. The head of the palace staff, by God's grace, liked Daniel, but he warned him, "I'm afraid of what my master the king will do. He is the one who assigned this diet and if he sees that you are not as healthy as the rest, he'll have my head!" (Daniel 1:8-10)

In the months since Daniel had been picked out in Jerusalem as a potential future leader, Ashpenaz had been increasingly impressed with the young man. When Daniel made his special request, Ashpenaz wanted to say "yes," but he couldn't. But he didn't say "no" either. He told Daniel, "I'm afraid if I let you do this I'll get in trouble."

Ashpenaz's response gave Daniel an opening for a creative alternative. Daniel had to figure out a way to avoid the king's table yet not get Ashpenaz in trouble. He had to analyze the situation. He realized that the real objective wasn't to eat the king's food; the real issue was glowing health. The king naturally assumed his food was the best. Daniel wasn't prepared to grant him that assumption. But if they didn't eat the king's food, what would they eat? They wouldn't stay healthy if they went on a hunger fast. A plan began to form in Daniel's mind. There was a way that the boys could eat, not violate their convictions, and still look as healthy as anyone eating from the king's table.

A creative alternative is a plan or strategy that allows you to meet your objective without causing a serious problem for someone else. Ashpenaz wasn't worried about Daniel's diet; he was worried about losing his life! He knew that Nebuchadnezzar would probably take offense if he caught his chief of palace staff deliberately disobeying his orders. He didn't want to make the king mad. Daniel had to come up with a plan that allowed him to maintain his own integrity but didn't endanger Ashpenaz.

Dan's strategy was simple, brilliant, and gave God room to work in the situation! Note what he did:

Daniel appealed to a steward who had been assigned by the head of the palace staff to be in charge of Daniel, Hananiah, Mishael, and Azariah: "Try us out for ten days on a simple diet of vegetables and water. Then compare us with the young men who eat from the royal menu. Make your decision on the basis of what you see."

The steward agreed to do it and fed them vegetables and water for ten days. At the end of the ten days they looked better and more robust than all the others who had been eating from the royal menu. So the steward continued to exempt them from the royal menu of food and drink and served them only vegetables. (verses 11-16)

Problem solved. The key to coming up with a creative alternative is to think about what everyone in the situation really wants. Ashpenaz wanted a happy king and healthy students. The steward needed to have healthy eaters so he wouldn't get in trouble with Ashpenaz. And Daniel and his friends wanted to please God. So the plan was a "conditional solution." It asked the question: If we can reach the same or even better results another way, can we at least try it temporarily? Some scholars think that part of the incentive for the steward was that he would still collect helpings from the king's buffet for the Jewish boys but would eat them himself, while he supplied Daniel and his friends with the food he was supposed to eat. That way, no one but the steward and the young men would know what was happening, yet everyone's purposes would be met. The plan worked! The little Hebrew fraternity members were even healthier than their classmates who had been feasting at the king's buffet.

Creative alternatives need to be stated respectfully and graciously. They are not guaranteed to succeed, but they often do. Again, there are times in life when we must be prepared to say "no" and deal with the stress that brings. But more often than we suspect, we may be able to live in peace with others if we figure out what they really want and show them a way to get it that doesn't require us to do something we believe God does not want us to do.

This area of creative alternatives is one of the proving grounds of wisdom. It may be helpful to think about situations that could require this kind of approach. Again, you will be practicing decision-making ahead of time. Some of this may be a requirement right now in your life. What if your friends invite you to a graduation party where the "buffet" might be loaded with stuff that fits in the defilement category for you—under-age drinking, illegal drugs, sexual activities that are completely inappropriate for people outside of marriage? If, like Daniel and his friends, you've made the decision not to defile yourself, you may be able to completely avoid many of those environments. But what if you find yourself in a potentially compromising situation (the stress meter just went into the red zone)? What are your creative alternative options?

The obvious plan is to immediately and politely excuse yourself because you need to be somewhere else. But that may not always be practical. If you've driven with someone else, you may have to deal with the "stuck" factor. Take a look around you. Ask God for X-ray vision. You will probably be able to see at least one other person who is also looking for a way *not* to participate. Approach that person and say something like, "I don't know about you, but this little event is outside my comfort zone. How are you doing?" You haven't asked that person to risk exposure until you have risked it. It shouldn't take you more than a couple of tries to locate a kindred spirit to hang out with, maybe making your way to neutral territory. When you take a small step on the journey toward living a self-controlled life, you will be amazed how often others are relieved to join you. Jesus mixed it up with all kinds of people, but he never allowed others to determine what he was going to do in any situation. Pattern your life after his, and you'll always know you're in good company.

5

Stepping Over Fault Lines and Potholes
(Work-Related, Money-Related, and God-Related Stress)

Graduation from Babel On U meant that Dan and his friends were ushered as rookies into the ranks of Babylonian wise men and counselors. The king may have been impressed with their showing during oral examination, but the hierarchy of established "magicians and enchanters" (Daniel 1:20) probably didn't think very highly of the young upstarts from the little land of Israel. There may have been an active effort to keep distance between Daniel and the king. And since Dan and his friends were not exactly knocking down walls and taking no prisoners to get ahead, they dropped out of sight. As long as everything went forward as usual, the latest class of graduates had little opportunity to shine. That's exactly what the established group wanted to accomplish. Anyone who outshone them as much as the Hebrew scholars had under the king's examination was a threat to them. They might be under the king's special protection, but that didn't prevent their rivals who were in charge from keeping them busy with pointless tasks and menial work.

Life out in the world can be a shocking dose of reality. You may get great ACT scores and grades your senior year of high school, but when you hit college, you will be a lowly freshman. Your schedule will be filled with introductory classes. You'll have to prove yourself academically all over again. Fast-forward four years and the same thing will happen again. You may go from campus wiz kid to the low person on the intern ladder in a firm. Your chance to demonstrate your abilities may come at any time. The question for you will be, "Should I stress over not getting noticed or not getting ahead fast enough or should I focus on doing outstanding work in whatever tasks are assigned to me, trusting all along that God's interested in my career path and has good things in store for me?" When things don't seem to be going according to the plan you imagined, keep in mind that God's plans always work out! Write out Jeremiah 29:11 on a card and post it somewhere in plain sight as a reminder: "I know what I'm doing. I have it all planned out—plans to take care of you, not abandon you, plans to give you the future you hope for." After you write it out, go ahead and sign it, *God*.

Plans are good practices. They keep us on track and headed in the right direction. But plans are also fallible, especially when we don't ask for God's input from the beginning. They can get sidetracked, slowed down, or radically changed. But having a plan that gets altered is better than having no plan at all and no idea where you are headed! God doesn't waste time steering parked cars, but he does great things with vehicles that are on the move. Ask God to make it clear when the plans you are making do not line up with his will for you and to use the plans you make for his purpose. Remember, sometimes we see a different outcome for the plan than God does, and we cause ourselves stress when we worry about plans that don't work out. Better to plan and do what we can and leave the ultimate results to God. Proverbs 16 has some great wisdom on how plans fit into life. Here's a sample:

- Mortals make elaborate plans, but GOD has the last word (verse 1).
- Put GOD in charge of your work, then what you've planned will take place (verse 3).
- We plan the way we want to live, but only GOD makes us able to live it (verse 9).

So go ahead, make a plan for college. Create a plan for life. Present it to God and give him the freedom to alter it for the better. Then start watching what will happen!

Here are some good questions to think about as you include God in your plans for life and college: Does God want me to go to college? If he wants me to go to college, should I expect him to show me that in part by providing a way for me to go to school? The deeper issue here is including God in your future plans, even if they seem like no-brainer choices. Don't expect God to help you in this area if you haven't given him a chance to do so. At the very least, keep yourself open to the possibility that God's plan for you includes school in a way you couldn't anticipate. Ask him to be your number one college and life adviser!

For example, you and a high percentage of people your age are clueless about how they are going to afford college. The assumption today is not whether it is a good idea to go into debt to finance an education; the only question seems to be, Where do I borrow the money? Other questions might be better to answer first: If I have to borrow money for school, should I go to school? What are some creative alternatives to fund education without debt? Military service is an option; work as you go is another. It's also good to ask, Have I exhausted all the possible sources of grants and other help? Loading up on debt may seem like an easy solution because it tries to shift the stress to the future—but how much control do we have over the future? We live during a time when those we have trusted to govern our lives have chosen for years to avoid difficult choices by going deeper and deeper into debt. Millions are trying this same approach on a smaller scale by borrowing for education based on the hope/confidence that they will get a great job after school and pay off the debts in no time. But there's something daunting, crushing, and, yes, stressful about getting your diploma from college and a bill in the mail that reminds you the bank expects their $100,000 back with interest.

Having to postpone or slow down college plans may seem stressful, but it doesn't compare to the weight of indentured servanthood for years, particularly if you spend four years and all that money to get a degree you can't use. It's kind of like signing a note for thousands of dollars for your dream car and wrecking it on the way home before you took out insurance. You can't drive that car; it's worthless, and you still have to pay back what you borrowed to get what is now a pile of metal, rubber, and plastic. Ask God to show you the best way to pay for school, and take to heart what he tells you.

Babylon Palace Mail Room

Meanwhile, back in Babylon, God had a plan for Dan and his friends. And even though it looked like they were stuck at the bottom of the pile, they waited patiently while the world above them seemed to move on. They were certainly not "on call" in the wise hierarchy of the palace.

Then the king had a dream. At first, this was great news to the magicians, enchanters, sorcerers, and fortune-tellers of Babylon. Dreams were their bread and butter. Generations had made careers out of coming up with clever explanations for the dreams that were presented to them. Their safety was in the lack of precision in the interpretation of dreams. They assumed the king's visions would be their ticket into assured roles in the highest levels of government. Not so fast, there, wise guys.

Some translations of the Bible make it seem as if Nebuchadnezzar had a troubling dream, but the only thing he could remember was that it was troubling. He forgot the details. So when he brought in the MESF crowd (magicians, enchanters, sorcerers, and fortune-tellers), they were shocked by his orders: "All right, boys. If you're worth all this money I'm paying you, then you can tell me not only what my dreams mean but also what I actually dreamed, because I can't really remember it." This explanation makes the king fairly simple-minded. But other clues indicate the young ruler was pretty sharp.

Another translation implies that the king remembered vividly what he dreamed, and he even had a pretty good idea what it meant. So he decided to test all the people around him whom he suspected didn't have a clue about the wisdom, foreknowledge, and insight they claimed.

The MESF took their usual approach and got into their profound and scholarly listening mode: "Go ahead, king, tell us the dream and we'll unpack it for you." They were sure if they got a hint of the dream, they could come up with some kind of impressive explanation.

Instead of describing his dream, the king issued a threat along with a carrot on a stick:

> The king answered the fortunetellers, "This is my decree: If you can't tell me both the dream itself and its interpretation, I'll have you ripped to pieces, limb from limb, and your homes torn down. But if you tell me both the dream and its interpretation, I'll lavish you with gifts and honors. So go to it: Tell me the dream and its interpretation." (Daniel 2:5-6)

The MESF pretended they didn't hear that last little bit and continued their standard operating procedure: "We're ready for the gifts and honors, king. Just tell us the dream, and we will amaze you with an interpretation." They weren't prepared to be challenged on their own turf. Their skills weren't supposed to be questioned. Meanwhile, Dan and the boys were down in the mail room, sorting packages, oblivious to the storm clouds gathering overhead.

Nebuchadnezzar was going to do more than test his MESF; he was about to blow their cover and even take their lives.

> The king said, "I know what you're up to — you're just playing for time. You know you're up a tree. You know that if you can't tell me my dream, you're doomed. I see right through you — you're going to cook up some fancy stories and confuse the issue until I change my mind. Nothing doing! First tell me the dream, then I'll know that you're on the up and up with the interpretation and not just blowing smoke in my eyes." (verses 8-9)

The king had them and he knew it. They knew it, too.

In a desperate attempt to save their skins, the MESF decided to try the truth:

> "Nobody anywhere can do what you ask. And no king, great or small, has ever demanded anything like this from any magician, enchanter, or fortuneteller. What you're asking is impossible unless some god or goddess should reveal it — and they don't hang around with people like us." (verses 10-11)

They were saying, "Now we know what you're asking, king, and frankly it's a first. We can't answer and no one can unless they have information that can only come from a god—and none of us has those kinds of contacts."

The king's next words were basically, "Take a memo. To my execution squad. I want every member of the MESF killed today. They are worthless."

When the memo arrived in the mail room for distribution, Dan and his friends realized the news was bad. Even as rookie members of the MESF, their goose was cooked, too. They hadn't even been invited to the showdown with the king, but they were not going to be overlooked when the heads rolled! This is probably a good note to keep in mind as you prepare to move into the workforce yourself. The good stuff often doesn't trickle down as far as the bad stuff. In fact, sometimes the bad stuff starts at the bottom and works its way up! You can figure that Daniel and his friends would have been invited to be at the front of the line for the beheadings. The important thing to remember, however, is that Daniel kept his head when the stress reared its ugly one. Things looked as bad as they could be, but Daniel had been on the sidelines until that point. He just knew that God's plan for them didn't end with the mail room in the palace.

Daniel went to Arioch, the man in charge of the upcoming executions of the MESF, and found out what had caused the king to speed-dial the exterminators. Once he got the story straight, he went to the king and asked for a little time, after which he promised to deliver exactly what the king had asked for. Intrigued that at least one member of the MESF seemed to be competent, the king granted Daniel's request.

Talk about stress! At this point, Daniel had absolutely no idea what the king had dreamed. But he did know that God knew, and that the only hope for the entire MESF crew was if God was willing to part with the knowledge. So, he immediately called in backup. He gathered his three friends for a serious prayer meeting.

A candid conversation with the living God, who created the universe and sustains it without breaking a sweat, is the best medicine for stress. You don't need a prescription for this treatment. But it helps to practice often. When you get in the habit of talking to God about everything, it feels like the most natural thing in the world to turn to him when everything hits the fan!

But this can't be some nursery rhyme, now-I-lay-me-down-to-sleep, Lord-please-preserve-me-from-that-creep or some such prayer. You've got to have a heart-to-heart talk with the God who has plans for you. Notice how Daniel put it to his friends: "He asked them to pray to the God of heaven for mercy in solving this mystery so that the four of them wouldn't be killed along with the whole company of Babylonian wise men" (verse 18). Praying as if your life depended on it is a good habit to develop—because sometimes it does. That attitude helps you stay in touch with the fact that your life doesn't belong to you and you really don't control tomorrow. Once you take God's mercy into account, you will be amazed how much less stress will affect you. You are no longer trying to control things that are really God's responsibility. Let God take that load off your shoulders.

God revealed to Daniel the dream and its meaning. He had Arioch issue a temporary stay of execution and showed up in the king's presence. Having humiliated the entire MESF team, Nebuchadnezzar was a little doubtful that Dan could deliver. This gave Dan a great opportunity to shine the spotlight of the moment where it belonged — on God.

> Daniel answered the king, "No mere human can solve the king's mystery. I don't care who it is — no wise man, enchanter, magician, diviner. But there is a God in heaven who solves mysteries, and he has solved this one. He is letting King Nebuchadnezzar in on what is going to happen in the days ahead. This is the dream you had when you were lying on your bed, the vision that filled your mind." (verses 27–28)

Dan then went on to describe the dream and explain its meaning. He made it clear that God and God alone was giving Nebuchadnezzar a glimpse into the future. The dream and interpretation are found in Daniel 2:29-45. The sequence of rising and falling world powers foretold in Nebuchadnezzar's dream can be seen in the history books. It is so accurate that modern people who have a somewhat dim view of God's role in things have a difficult time accepting that God gave away history before it happened. But remember this: Problems people have with the Bible are always problems people have with God. A failure to know God leads to a failure to appreciate his Word. It isn't surprising that people who decide that God, whoever he is, can't know the future, or work miracles, or control events around the world also can't accept the Bible, which clearly describes God doing all of those things and more. Whether it has been easy or hard for you to trust God and see the Bible as his reliable source of communication with you, realize that as you move out on your own, you are sure to encounter a lot of people who are quite definite in their unbelief. They think they have found some kind of substitute for the God in heaven that works for them, and they can be quite belligerent if you dare to point out, even gently, that their god can't hold a candle to the God who has revealed himself in the Bible and as Jesus Christ.

When Daniel described God "in heaven who solves mysteries," he was also reminding us that God is the ultimate mystery. We would know nothing about God if he did not choose to reveal himself to us. If we could figure God out on our own and contain him in our minds, he would be a limited god, someone we would have real problems trusting. But the God of the Bible, who revealed clues about himself in creation, in us, and ultimately by his personal visit to creation (see Romans 1; Hebrews 1), is so great and beyond our full comprehension that we simply have to trust him. The experience of believers all the way back to the time of Daniel and far beyond is not that people understand God so they trust him, but that people come to trust God and then grow in their understanding.

God has to be big enough to explain everything. Writer and teacher C. S. Lewis stated on several occasions that he had come to believe in the God of Christianity like he believed in the sun, not only because he could see it but because by it he could see everything else. Another writer, G. K. Chesterton, put this same insight a different way:

> It is very hard for a man to defend anything of which he is entirely convinced. It is comparatively easy when he is only partially convinced. He is partially convinced because he has found this or that proof of the thing, and he can expound it. But a man is not really convinced of a philosophic theory when he finds that *something* proves it. He is only really convinced when he finds that *everything* proves it.[2]

That's why, when people try to come up with a substitute for God, they invent a god or an explanation that is supposed to cover everything else. When you realize this, it helps you see what small little gods people invent to avoid trusting the God in heaven. For example, the big bang theory is seriously introduced as a scientific explanation for everything (as well as a really great excuse for not having to include God in creation). The "big bang" is, for some people, the central mystery that makes all else make sense. Whatever "banged" and where it came from is part of the mystery, so it remains largely on its own in the far distant past. They unknowingly try to rewrite Genesis 1, substituting "big bang" each place God is mentioned. Something like, "In the beginning, the big bang resulted in the heavens and the earth . . ." The phrase "created the heavens and the earth" doesn't work because it smuggles in a thinking, creating Actor, and the whole point of the big bang is to remove any possibility of a deliberate, personal Creator responsible for everything.

The real problem with every substitute for God, or even the denial of God, is that it also makes the one creating the substitute or denying God equally meaningless. A theory like the big bang isn't a big enough mystery to explain everything because it fails miserably to explain *you*. It may offer you the heart-warming explanation that you are an inconvenient, incidental accident in the evolutionary process, but using that explanation as a reason that gives life purpose is so *not* satisfactory! You were not designed to easily accept the stress of believing that life has no meaning. God mixed that stress into you when he created you as one of the experiences that could drive you back to him. Maybe you can identify with something Saint Augustine pointed out many centuries ago in a prayer that went something like, "Our hearts are always restless until they find their rest in you." If you recognize that restlessness in yourself, realize you will only find that profound inner rest when you surrender your life into God's hands.

Meanwhile, Back at the Castle

When Daniel was finished with this analysis of the dream, the king was literally floored! Nebuchadnezzar realized that Daniel was getting his information from a source beyond human capabilities, just as Daniel himself had told him. The king said, "Your God is beyond question the God of all gods, the Master of all kings. And he solves all mysteries, I know, because you've solved this mystery" (Daniel 2:47). This was a pretty large admission for someone who was being told every day that he was the ruler of the world! And, as we will see in the next chapter, Nebuchadnezzar had a long way to go before he applied the reality of God's existence to his own life.

But this episode brought about big changes for Dan and his friends. Daniel received gifts from the king and was made "governor over the entire province of Babylon and the chief in charge of all the Babylonian wise men" (verse 48). He went from being buried in the mail room to the main chair in the boardroom. And Daniel immediately requested that the king assign positions in government to Shadrach, Meshach, and Abednego. They all moved to the head of the class. This wasn't something they schemed to do; God's plan just took another step forward.

You Never Know

As you move out into this new adventure in life, you don't know what each day will bring. Some days will devastate you; others will elevate you. Various kinds of stress will swirl through your relationships, your work, and even your inner life. Often, the crises in other people's lives will allow you to practice trusting God, which is one good reason to keep your relationship with God up to date.

When Dan and his friends showed up for work that morning, they didn't know that they would be dealing with the stress of a life-threatening royal command by the end of the day. They didn't realize that they would be raised way up in standing and responsibility within hours. Daniel didn't know that every member of the MESF would owe their lives to him. He didn't know that the people whose lives he saved would eventually scheme to try to get rid of him. There was a whole pile of things he didn't know.

Your days are exactly the same. The context is different, and you're more likely to deal with a superior at work than with the president of the country, but even that is possible. The fact that you don't know what will happen today and tomorrow puts you in the same situation that Dan and his friends faced. So, what kept them and what can keep you from becoming completely stressed out about not knowing? The answer is remembering that you know Someone who *does* know. God knows your tomorrow better than you know your yesterday. He knows what you will need each moment of your unfolding life, and he will supply what you need as you trust him.

What does that mean—trusting God with what you don't know? Since every new day is a "you don't know" experience, each day is also an opportunity to tell God you're going to trust him as you move through the events of the day. When unexpected delights happen, you can think, *God knew about this and decided to surprise me—thank you, Lord.*

When sudden difficulties of all kinds come along, you can think, *God knew this was going to happen, and he will help me get through it—thank you, Lord.*

Psalm 139 is a great statement about the way God relates to us. One of the areas that it covers beautifully is the way God knows us and our future. You may feel like your future is an exciting blank page to be filled in—and in many ways it is. But from God's perspective, your future is an exciting itinerary that he already knows. David wrote,

> Oh yes, you shaped me first inside, then out;
>   you formed me in my mother's womb.
> I thank you, High God — you're breathtaking!
>   Body and soul, I am marvelously made!
>   I worship in adoration — what a creation!
> You know me inside and out,
>   you know every bone in my body;
> You know exactly how I was made, bit by bit,
>   how I was sculpted from nothing into something.
> Like an open book, you watched me grow from
>   conception to birth;
>   all the stages of my life were spread out before
>   you,
> The days of my life all prepared
>   before I'd even lived one day. (verses 13–16)

High or low, fast or slow, there's no place you will be today that God has not already been. When the unknown creates stress in your life, you don't have to let it knock you off your feet. Instead you can use it as a life reminder to turn to God again, no matter how many times you've already done it today, and say, "Thanks, Lord, for knowing where I'm going, and for going there with me!"

6

No Time to Be Idle Around Idols
(Insecurity, Nonconformity, and Stress)

If it had been big enough, you would have climbed *inside* your locker. Maybe stayed there the whole day. Then you could at least honestly say you were in school! You knew that when you shut the door and turned into the flow in the hallway, you were going to get looks and comments. High school hallways are often gauntlets of cruelty.

One group carries on a running assessment of each person's wardrobe as they walk by: "Shopping at Goodwill again, I see." Or you have to stroll the runway of the style police: "Did you actually look at yourself in a mirror before you left your house today? Is that a haircut, or did you just trip and fall under your dad's lawnmower?" Others have no mercy with the snide remarks about physical traits: "If that pimple blows, they'll have to declare the school a toxic waste site" or "Add three more pounds and you'll be a finalist for *The Biggest Loser*!"

The comments are crude and humiliating, and they drive us to avoid standing out in the crowd. We want to disappear. The spotlight of public ridicule is just too bright and hot for us.

You have probably already experienced the amazing power of peer pressure while you were in high school. It doesn't get any easier throughout life. The stress you experienced over "belonging" during the last few years has been your introduction to a variety of situations to come throughout your life when you will have to decide with whom you will stand. And whether or not we realize it, we are designed to stand best when we stand with others for good and clear reasons.

As you have learned, the pressure to conform can take almost opposite forms. On the one side, certain groups on campus can make life miserable for those who don't fit their idea of dress or behavior. But isn't it interesting how, on the other side, most of the nonconformists on campus all look and dress the same? In order to be known as unique rebels, people end up conforming to the current idea of how a nonconformist dresses and acts. So, it's not surprising to see the table groups in the cafeteria, where the jocks huddle, and the geeks network, the gamers compare scores, the social queens gossip, and even the uniquers gather to make sure that, by observing one another, they are still unique. Even nonconformists want to belong!

External signs like tattoos, earrings, shoe styles, and bandannas are treated as dependable clues about what makes people unusual, but they often fail to tell the truth. People are posers all the time. And frankly, one of the built-in experiences of high school is trying on various personal styles to see how they fit. Since we often don't have a clear idea of who we are, we end up experimenting with "types" during these years. This is just part of the journey unless we get to the end and all we've got is a person we're pretending to be instead of discovering who we are.

It's hard to spot a true nonconformist. Since the subtle pokes to "go along" are all around us, the nonconformist isn't necessarily someone whose goal is to be different in every situation. That kind of person is just a different kind of human chameleon. One kind of human chameleon conforms to whatever situation they are in — their only compass is what's going on around them. Their language, behavior, and even thought patterns morph into something that fits where they are at the moment. This is the kind of person who has people at home convinced that they are simply the next generation of the family while at the same time convincing people at school that they are the poster child for the latest version of their group personality. If someone from either environment observed that person in their alternate setting, they would be shocked. They might not even recognize the chameleon. Ask yourself, Would the people who know me in different places in my life say I'm the same person if they met me in one of my other locations?

The other kind of human chameleon is just as influenced by circumstances, but they try hard to do, be, and say something other than the norm that surrounds them. They don't care what they are doing as long as they can say, "See, I'm different. I'm not like the rest of you." But put them in another group minutes later, and they will change almost instantly to be different again. Instead of shifting to become *like*, they shift to become *unlike*—no matter what the actual results.

What both kinds of human chameleons have in common is that their lives are entirely governed by their circumstances. They are rarely themselves. They may not even have a clue about who they are because their only mirrors are the expectations of others.

The apostle Paul, who lived hundreds of years after Daniel and his friends, gave us a golden nugget of insight into what it means to be a genuine and godly nonconformist.

> Don't become so well-adjusted to your culture that you fit into it without even thinking. Instead, fix your attention on God. You'll be changed from the inside out. Readily recognize what he wants from you, and quickly respond to it. Unlike the culture around you, always dragging you down to its level of immaturity, God brings the best out of you, develops well-formed maturity in you. (Romans 12:2)

We've already seen the genuine nonconformist response in Daniel and his friends when they were invited to enjoy the king's buffet. That's an example of the selective way that conformity comes at us. Giving in doesn't usually present itself as a do-or-die confrontation. The cultural tactic is to "go along" to get along. But sometimes the world comes at us with an overwhelming frontal attack. The stress level can go from close to zero to the top of the scale pretty quickly. If being, to use Paul's term, "well-adjusted to your culture" means that you have been "going along" without really thinking about the direction or consequences, you may be overwhelmed by the sudden pressure to surrender in ways you weren't expecting.

The desire to belong that we discussed earlier in this chapter can be negative or positive. We were not actually designed to live completely independent of others. Once we know who we are and the way we want to live, there is great strength in discovering others who share the same outlook and values. If you are headed off to college as a Christian in a non-Christian environment, you can fully expect to experience both subtle and harsh stress to conform away from Christian values. You will be invited and even harassed into accepting *any* alternative worldview as long as it is not the Christian worldview. You may feel you're alone. But beyond the obvious truth that God is with you, there will undoubtedly be other Christians around you who are struggling with the same pressures you are. Make it a priority to locate them. Check out the Christian groups on campus. You will be amazed how tempting it will be to become well-adjusted to the culture on your campus by setting aside what you know to be true. Don't wait to discover others who will encourage you and stand with you in preserving the special work that God is doing in your life.

Dan and his three friends survived their years of college by standing together. By remaining true from the start at the king's table, they didn't have to try to go back and rebuild their integrity or their relationship with God. They kept things current all along the way. We don't know the details of the situations they overcame, but they probably parallel many of the circumstances you will face on your own. The lesson to remember from this small band of four guys is that it's better to go through a tough challenge in the right way and live with integrity than to go through it in the wrong way and live with regrets.

Also, the absence of details during their training years is a good reminder that while the day-to-day experiences during the first years away from home may drag on and feel endless as we are living through them, looking back it will be amazing how quickly they passed. Too many people give up because they think that the stress won't end. It's better to look at the various pressures you will face with the one-day-at-a-time approach. If you spend too much time worrying about how long this will go, you won't pay careful enough attention to the immediate issues you need to deal with. Jesus was exactly right when he said,

> People who don't know God and the way he works fuss over these things, but you know both God and how he works. Steep your life in God-reality, God-initiative, God-provisions. Don't worry about missing out. You'll find all your everyday human concerns will be met.
>
> Give your entire attention to what God is doing right now, and don't get worked up about what may or may not happen tomorrow. God will help you deal with whatever hard things come up when the time comes. (Matthew 6:32-34)

Because stressful times come in so many shapes and sizes, you need to have a default plan that's bigger than whatever is causing stress. Knowing "God and the way he works" is that strategy. The day-by-day approach we mentioned above is best carried out with an everyday awareness of God's place in our lives. No matter how steady and free from stress your days might seem, God has a role in them. He's just as much in charge when it's smooth sailing as he is when the storms come. The best use of the calm seas is learning to trust God. Think about Jesus' phrase above, "Steep your life in God-reality, God initiative, God-provisions." If some of those terms are a little unfamiliar, start by considering what it means to you that God is always there, always first, and always faithful. *Steep* is a word used primarily in tea-making, but it conveys the picture of soaking or saturating. The idea is to learn that God really is present and aware of everything going on in our lives. That way, when something unexpected happens to us, the first thought can be that it wasn't unexpected to God.

Daniel and his friends discovered this lesson early on, and their later lives show us that the approach didn't fail them. As you think about your life at this moment, how "steeped" are you when it comes to God's role in the events that are going on? Is graduation about you or is it about him? In what ways can you honestly say that you have arrived at the place you are today because God has made it possible? As we will see, the boys in Babylon understood that every achievement that came their way started with God's faithfulness.

Babel U on Graduation Day

So, the foursome from Jerusalem made it to graduation day. They did well in school. The summary account of their educational experience is as follows:

God gave these four young men knowledge and skill in both books and life. In addition, Daniel was gifted in understanding all sorts of visions and dreams. At the end of the time set by the king for their training, the head of the royal staff brought them in to Nebuchadnezzar. When the king interviewed them, he found them far superior to all the other young men. None were a match for Daniel, Hananiah, Mishael, and Azariah.

And so they took their place in the king's service. Whenever the king consulted them on anything, on books or on life, he found them ten times better than all the magicians and enchanters in his kingdom put together. (Daniel 1:17-20)

The final exams must have been a little stressful. Imagine the memo from the college president Dan and his friends found in their mailboxes: "Attention upperclassmen: For your last assignment, you will be ushered before King Nebuchadnezzar for a personal interview and testing. Don't make us look bad. Just remember that the king's grade isn't just pass or fail; it's pass or die! But relax and have a good time. No pressure."

The boys not only passed their graduation test, but they passed the life test. Notice that Nebuchadnezzar "consulted" them "on books or on life" and found that they had practical answers. They stood out from the crowd. They had mastered the material they were supposed to learn in school, but they also demonstrated they could *think*. They answered questions with learned facts, but they also offered insights that came out of their understanding that God is central to life.

Now you may be wondering, *I thought that's what I'm going to school to learn to do—think*. Hopefully, thinking is something you already know how to do. College will give you new things to think about but not necessarily teach you how to think. Often, school becomes an isolated environment where questions are actually controlled. The standard method of education is to insist that you question everything you have learned up until then. But (and watch this carefully), often the tone and direction of the questions won't be to figure out how and why the things you have learned until now are true; the point will be to prove that everything in your past is somehow false or at best less significant than what you are about to learn.

If the central value of your life is God, expect to have that value seriously challenged in college. Don't be surprised if you hear faith mocked. But here's the key thought to keep in mind: What are they offering as a suitable replacement? The world doesn't have anything to offer that compares with God. The only thing the world can do is try to minimize and miniaturize God so that he seems just as insignificant and incapable as whatever they have to offer instead of him. And just so you know, the world will offer you a human system to replace God. All that the world has to offer is something far less than God—it's an offer not worth taking. But in the insulated environment that school can be, that offer may seem tempting. Especially if you haven't mastered the drive to belong that we considered earlier in this chapter.

Working 9 to 5

Sooner or later, the challenges are going to come. At least once in your life the issue of who you really trust is going to be forced into the open. In one way or another, situations are going to show up that give you a clear opportunity to demonstrate your trust in God or discover that you actually trust something or someone other than God. In the lives of Shadrach, Meshach, and Abednego, the big showdown came a few years after school. By then, they were settled into careers as government officials in Babylon.

Although he should have known better, Nebuchadnezzar let his own power and success go to his head (and it wasn't the only time, either). People around him did everything they could to preserve the illusion of kingly divinity. The king may have been exercising a faulty memory of a dream God had given him years before (see chapter 8), but the result was an amazing statue of Nebuchadnezzar's likeness, covered in gold, displayed on the plain of Dura. Apparently, the large flat area made the gigantic image (ninety feet high) visible from a distance.

Kings have always built large objects to give themselves a sense of permanence and greatness. The pyramids are some of the largest, and certainly most elaborate, gravestones ever erected. But kings have also gone beyond seeing themselves as leaders to see themselves as gods. And somewhere along the way, Nebuchadnezzar's huge statue was designated an object to be worshipped. Then, as an incentive toward full participation, the crowd was told that anyone who didn't obey the musical signal and bow before the statue would be cooked alive in a furnace. Standing out under the sun on the plain of Dura must have been hot enough to convince most people that a trip to the furnace was a destination worth avoiding. So the crowd bowed.

Like a wheat field bending in the wind, as the first sounds of the orchestra reached the people, waves of human bodies folded. It may have taken a few moments for someone to realize that three people were still on their feet. Talk about standing out in a crowd!

Whoever peeked set off the alarm. As soon as the musical bowing period was over, accusers turned in Shadrach, Meshach, and Abednego as rebels.

> They said to King Nebuchadnezzar, "Long live the king! You gave strict orders, O king, that when the big band started playing, everyone had to fall to their knees and worship the gold statue, and whoever did not go to their knees and worship it had to be pitched into a roaring furnace. Well, there are some Jews here — Shadrach, Meshach, and Abednego — whom you have placed in high positions in the province of Babylon. These men are ignoring you, O king. They don't respect your gods and they won't worship the gold statue you set up."
> (Daniel 3:9-12)

Our heroes were in trouble. The obvious first question for most of us is, Where was Daniel? If we look at the whole story and see who was invited to the unveiling of the statue, we discover that this was somewhat of a local event in the province of Babylon, not a nationwide convocation. It's quite possible that Daniel's duties kept him back at the palace while the king went out to be worshipped by the people who had gathered on the plain of Dura. It doesn't appear that this was a traveling statue, so the regional dedication of the icon might have been designed as the first in a series of by-invitation-only opportunities to declare loyalty to the king by bowing before the idol. The three Hebrews said, "No thanks."

This crisis may have occurred as long as fifteen years after Dan's three friends graduated from their elite training, and there's little indication that Nebuchadnezzar had direct contact with them after he assigned them to help govern the provinces. Since things were running smoothly under Shadrach, Meshach, and Abednego, the king probably didn't invite them for coffee on a weekly basis. Those who brought the accusation did so with cunning. They reminded the king of his "strict orders" before they informed him who had broken them. The king was furious. We're not sure what made him more angry: that someone had blatantly disobeyed him or that he was about to roast three of his prize governors. We get some hint of the king's dilemma since he brought in the three men but gave them a second chance. Nebuchadnezzar didn't want to lose these effective servants, but he didn't want to lose face either.

We interrupt this dramatic moment with a wisdom note. When you do get work, it's wise to work with diligence and integrity. You don't have to overdo it to ingratiate yourself with your bosses—doing a good job is your best statement of value. When you do get promoted, consider the opportunity in light of what you know of your abilities. Being able to do a job well is probably better than getting more money and responsibility for a job you do poorly. If you're not sure you can handle more responsibility, say so. Appreciate the new job offer but tell the boss you would like to be as effective in the new role as you were in the old, but you're not entirely sure that will be the case. Then ask if it would be possible to return to your current job in six months if either you or the boss doesn't feel you're up to the new role. This might be a good example of a creative alternative we discussed in chapter 4.

And now, back to the unfolding stressful moment. Even though the king gave Shadrach, Meshach, and Abednego a second chance, they remained respectfully and literally unbending. Basically they said, "King, we think big band music is great for dancing, but not for bowing." After all, the king not only made the issue personal, he also made it spiritual when he ended his threat with, "Who is the god who can rescue you from my power?" (verse 15). He should have known better.

The full answer by the friends was firm but respectful:

Shadrach, Meshach, and Abednego answered King Nebuchadnezzar, "Your threat means nothing to us. If you throw us in the fire, the God we serve can rescue us from your roaring furnace and anything else you might cook up, O king. But even if he doesn't, it wouldn't make a bit of difference, O king. We still wouldn't serve your gods or worship the gold statue you set up." (verses 16–18)

To our modern ears so used to being berated about tolerance, these calm words of uncompromising integrity sound almost prideful. We like to think we're open-minded and fair, when in fact we find it difficult to hold our ground faced with minimal pressure. If something is true, then we shouldn't be willing to say it's untrue no matter how we are threatened. Dan's friends stood their ground, not because they were sure they would survive the furnace but because they knew honoring God with their lives was more important than temporarily preserving their lives!

The answer to that stressful confrontation according to today's culture would probably be that the boys should have bowed "on the outside" to get along while on the inside they were still standing for God. But sooner or later we have to decide what we will live for, and those beliefs we must also be willing to die for. We are far more likely to be threatened with embarrassment or loss of position than loss of life, yet we rarely show the kind of backbone that Daniel's friends displayed. When push came to ultimate shove, they said, "We will serve you, king, as we always have, but our ultimate allegiance is to God. That's our story, and we're sticking to it. Bring on the oven."

It's possible that Nebuchadnezzar couldn't remember anyone ever standing up to him that way. His rage got the best of him. He ordered the furnace to be super-heated. Then he assigned elite soldiers to tie up Shadrach, Meshach, and Abednego, who were not resisting, and toss them into the flames. Unfortunately, the furnace was such a raging inferno that the soldiers who delivered Dan's friends to the opening suffered fatal burns themselves. Meanwhile, the three men fell into the roaring fire and hopped to their feet, since the restraining ropes immediately burned away. They were at least as cool as the people waiting around under the sun. Not a hair was singed and even their clothes remained undamaged.

As shocking as the survival of his servants was, Nebuchadnezzar was even more stunned to clearly see a fourth figure strolling in the furnace with the men who worshipped the God of Israel: "'But look!' he said. 'I see four men, walking around freely in the fire, completely unharmed! And the fourth man looks like a son of the gods!'" (verse 25). This is the only time the fourth man is mentioned in the story. God was certainly present for those three faithful men. Bible scholars have frequently suggested that this was Jesus showing up in a special way. If it was, then he fulfilled something he promised before he even made the promise to his disciples: "And when two or three of you are together because of me, you can be sure that I'll be there" (Matthew 18:20).

Alone or with good friends, it isn't easy to stand up in stressful situations. We don't go looking for them. But when they come at us, one of the amazing possibilities is that as we face difficulties in our efforts to represent God, we will experience his presence in special ways right in the middle of the stress. Those who are watching us and wondering why God would let us go through such a tough time will definitely have something to think about when God helps us survive and thrive despite the difficulties we face.

When he saw what God did for Shadrach, Meshach, and Abednego, the king realized that when it came to real divinity, he was a little boy playing in a sandbox. He wasn't sure what to say, so he made an observation using his frame of reference: "There has never been a god who can pull off a rescue like this" (Daniel 3:29). The main thing Nebuchadnezzar demonstrated with this statement was that he had little idea who this God was who was dealing with him. But God wasn't finished with him.

The pathway of your life will cross others' lives, and some of those people will wield a lot of power over you. At times it may seem overwhelming. But keep remembering that God is greater. He is greater in a whole different category of greatness. If you will keep your attention on him in the hard times ahead, you will experience "rescues" that amaze even you.

Bad News, Good News
(Losses and Friends Who Won't Listen)

Even caller ID doesn't prevent some bad news from getting through. You recognize the number as a safe one to answer—your sister is calling. But when you say, "Hello," there's a deep sigh on the other end, and then you hear a familiar voice say, "We had to take Dad to the hospital today. It doesn't look good." Phone ringing, low level of stress; but a parent dying provokes a very high level of stress. It's hard to get those calls, and it is hard to make them. As you move out into life on your own, you can expect that over the next few years you will have your share of hard calls to make and hard calls to take.

The more valuable the relationship, the more difficult it is to make and take hard calls. And yet life being as it is, those hard calls are all part of the package. That's what couples acknowledge (though they often don't think about it) when they say in their marriage vows, "For better or for worse, for richer or for poorer, in sickness and in health." We all want marriage to be about better, richer, and health. But we need to take into account the fact that life includes worse, poorer, and sickness.

Hospital Call

Pete stepped out of the delivery room. His shoulders were aching from hours of supporting his wife as she gave birth to their firstborn, a son. He thought for a moment about his efforts and then laughed over the insignificance of his work compared to the labor his wife had endured to bring a new life into the world. He knew he would never be able to even joke about suffering in the delivery process.

He pulled the list out of his pocket and checked. The phone number for his parents-in-law was at the top. They were waiting hundreds of miles away to get the news that their first grandchild was born. As he dialed their sequence, he wasn't sure exactly what he would say. The news seemed too good to put into words. As an indication of their anxiety, they both answered the phone together. When he heard their voices, Pete said, "Well, Mom and Dad, Sherrie came through with flying colors, and we have a little boy to raise. He's beautiful even after all the squeezing and pushing!"

He wasn't sure what the response would be, but he wasn't expecting silence. "Mom? Dad?" he asked, wondering if the connection had somehow been cut.

"We're here," his father-in-law said softly. "Are you sure

the baby is all right? Did they check everything?"

Pete was tempted for a moment to joke, "Yes, he's perfect! I counted all eleven toes myself!" But he sensed that his in-laws were worried for some reason, so he assured them the little boy was in good health and there was nothing wrong with him. The phone call so unnerved him that he was more subdued in the other calls he made—to his own parents and siblings, all of whom were becoming grandparents or aunts/uncles for the first time. One little baby was changing a crowd of identities!

When he returned to his wife, he shared that first conversation with her. "I'm not sure how your parents feel about their new and first grandson. They seemed more worried than happy," he concluded.

She lay quietly for a moment and then said, "I think they are reliving the past. They can't help it."

Pete asked, "What do you mean?"

"When my younger brother Bobbie was born, my parents were delighted! They were still hurting from my older sister's death due to a childhood sickness, and their first son and new baby was a fresh and hopeful start. Everything looked fine at first. But then he got sick and died too. I've seen pictures of me holding him as a tiny baby, but I don't actually remember him—I was too young. But I know that his death, along with my sister's, left them with a deep hurt that's still there."

"But how does that affect us?" Pete wondered out loud.

"It's hard for them not to think of events repeating themselves. Our little Matt looks healthy right now, but what if some kind of problem shows up tomorrow? I know they want to be happy for us, but they also remember their own hurts, and in a way they want to protect us."

Later, Pete wasn't surprised that Matt became a favorite of his grandparents, largely stemming from the way he grew to prove their fears and worries came to nothing.

Rough Places

Someone wisely noted that we tend to think of pleasure and good times as the smooth parts of life while pain and difficulties are seen as the rough stretches of travel. But that person also added, "Remember that on the journey up the mountain of life, if there weren't rough spots, we couldn't climb the slope. Smooth is all right for a rest, but if you want to get to the top, you've got to step on the rough spots that will keep your feet from slipping!"

One of the facts of life is that we tend to ignore the most important things, like God, when everything is going smoothly in life. But a few miles of bad road on life's journey can get our priorities back on track. God knows this about us. That's why he doesn't promise to keep hard things from us. He meets us in the rough places.

The people whose lives we've been following—Daniel, Shadrach, Meshach, Abednego, and Nebuchadnezzar—were all pretty close in age. The king was a little older, but he was still young when he took the throne of Babylon. So these five guys did a lot of growing together. Their relationship was more rough than smooth. But in particular, between Daniel and

Nebuchadnezzar, a friendship and trust developed. The king came to see over the years that he could count on Dan and his friends to always be truthful with him even if it was going to cost them.

When you consider the people you know and will know the longest in your life, how important has it been to treat them with integrity? Can they trust you? How do you know that? Have they been able to count on you during the rough spots of life, or have you been around as a friend only when the times were smooth? The rough spots are the stressful spots—the times when we need people around us we can trust who will walk with us farther up the mountain, helping one another climb. Life isn't just about you being able to survive stress; it's very much about you helping others to survive the stresses life hands them. How willing have you been to do that?

Another Dream

The king had another big dream. Instead of a huge, multilayered statue and a boulder, he saw a redwood-like tree towering over the landscape. The fourth chapter of Daniel is unique because most of it was written by Nebuchadnezzar himself, a report of an incredibly stressful time in his life.

After the dream, the king described it to his crowd of counselors. "None could tell me what it meant" (Daniel 4:7). Either the counselors were terrified over what the dream seemed to mean or they were simply clueless and didn't want to get the king angry again as they had years before. The dream (you can read the entire description in verses 10-17) starts with a big fruit tree that gets chopped down and capped with iron and bronze. Then the stump morphs into a human creature that lives among animals, even thinking like them for seven seasons. The closing of the dream gives some indication of why it might have been dangerous for a servant of the king to interpret it:

> The angels announce this decree,
>> the holy watchmen bring this sentence,
> So that everyone living will know
>> that the High God rules human kingdoms.
> He arranges kingdom affairs however he wishes,
>> and makes leaders out of losers. (verse 17)

In an age that suggested that human kings were divine, human counselors usually didn't risk reminding them that God was still in charge.

So Daniel was brought in to handle the king's vision. Nebuchadnezzar wrote, "It's your turn, Belteshazzar—interpret it for me. None of the wise men of Babylon could make heads or tails of it, but I'm sure you can do it. You're full of the divine Holy Spirit" (verse 18). Like the other members of the royal counselor's union, Dan was terrified by the interpretation of the dream. The cool-under-stress Daniel had to be reminded by his friend the king,

> "Belteshazzar," the king said, "stay calm. Don't let the dream and its interpretation scare you."

"My master," said Belteshazzar, "I wish this dream were about your enemies and its interpretation for your foes." (verse 19)

The king understood the dream well enough already to
promise Daniel he wouldn't hold him responsible for the bad
news contained in the message.

If you maintain relationships with people who don't share
your faith and you are honest about the way you are trying to
let God guide your life, don't be surprised if God uses them to
encourage your faith. People around you often listen better
than you think, and they have an uncanny way of reminding
you if you are acting in a way that is inconsistent with what you
claimed about you and God. Here Daniel was reminded by a
powerful king that he was representing Someone even more
powerful.

You Are the Tree

God wants to get us into a position where we acknowledge personal responsibility. You have grown up in a culture that
produces experts in blaming others. Few people wholeheart-
edly own up to the wrongs they do. But the Bible includes
numerous encounters with people to whom God gave the gift
of confrontation. God asks or tells people what he already
knows. He asked Adam and Eve, "Where are you?" even
though he could see where they were hiding. He asked Cain,
"What have you done?" even though he already knew Cain had
murdered his brother. God had Nathan tell King David a

parable that got the king very angry at the person in the story, and then Nathan looked him in the eye and said, "You're the man, David." God always wants to give us the best chance to own our behaviors and sins. Here Daniel described all the wonderful features of the tree and then added, "You, O king, are that tree" (verse 21).

If the tree represented the king, then the fate of the tree was the fate of the king. What awaited the king wasn't pretty.

> This, O king, also refers to you. It means that the High God has sentenced my master the king: You will be driven away from human company and live with the wild animals. You will graze on grass like an ox. You will be soaked in heaven's dew. This will go on for seven seasons, and you will learn that the High God rules over human kingdoms and that he arranges all kingdom affairs. (verses 24–25)

One very effective campaign slogan against the use of alcohol when driving included the punch line, "Friends don't let friends drive drunk." It stuck. Daniel was expressing a parallel slogan: "Friends don't let friends live proud." He also included the glimmer of good news for Nebuchadnezzar: Although it would take seven years to learn his lesson, the kingdom would be preserved and returned to him at that time. Even that would be a huge reminder that God is in charge.

Before the king could ask him what to do, Daniel gave him these instructions: "So, king, take my advice: Make a clean break with your sins and start living for others. Quit your wicked life and look after the needs of the down-and-out. Then *you* will continue to have a good life" (verse 27). Daniel was offering a way out. The dream was a picture of what would happen if things didn't change. King Nebuchadnezzar had plenty of reasons to not only recognize who God was but to seek to live his life by God's instructions. The second part was a problem. Up to this point in his life, the king had been forced to acknowledge God's existence several times. He had even told his people to submit to God. But he hadn't taken that step himself, even though he had the example of Daniel's life to demonstrate that God is fully able to handle our trust even in the toughest situations. What he could not say was, "No one ever warned me." In this way, Daniel was a true friend.

Remember that as stressful as it may be to warn friends about destructive patterns in their lives, the test of friendship isn't silence. And if a friend tries to tell us about a tendency he or she is seeing in our lives, it's a mark of friendship if we listen seriously. Friends can often see us better than we can see ourselves. As we said before, making and taking hard calls is stressful, but it's worth what can come out of them.

For Nebuchadnezzar, Daniel's warning was a passing moment. Twelve months later, while enjoying an evening of self-satisfaction and accomplishment, he crossed the line with God, boasting to those who were with him, "Look at this, Babylon the great! And I built it all by myself, a royal palace adequate to display my honor and glory!" (verse 30). Despite God's gift of a vivid warning vision, the king forgot that he was ruling under God's permission.

What happened next is quite remarkable. It's one of three

times when God makes a significant appearance in the book of Daniel.

> The words were no sooner out of his mouth than a voice out of heaven spoke, "This is the verdict on you, King Nebuchadnezzar: Your kingdom is taken from you. You will be driven out of human company and live with the wild animals. You will eat grass like an ox. The sentence is for seven seasons, enough time to learn that the High God rules human kingdoms and puts whomever he wishes in charge." (verses 31-32)

Being audibly interrupted by God would cause most people to come unhinged. It certainly sent Nebuchadnezzar over the edge. He immediately began acting so erratically and wildly that he was literally put out to pasture. He discovered firsthand the accuracy of the prediction in his vision. He could have written the book *My Seven Years as an Ox*, but he was too busy "ruminating."

At this point, Nebuchadnezzar picks up the story in his own words: "At the end of the seven years, I, Nebuchadnezzar, looked to heaven. I was given my mind back and I blessed the High God, thanking and glorifying God, who lives forever" (verse 34). When God was done with him, the king acknowledged that his whole experience, as hard as it had been *on* him, had also been good *for* him. His final words recorded in the book of Daniel are,

> Everything he does is right,
> and he does it the right way.

> He knows how to turn a proud person
>> into a humble man or woman. (verse 37)

Nebuchadnezzar gradually received a clearer and clearer picture of the King of Heaven. But we can't really be sure, based on the account in Daniel, that the king crossed the divide and placed his eternal destiny in God's hands. But he was never closer to starting a genuine relationship with God than when he was thoroughly humbled by the circumstances in his life.

Stress Tests

Eugene Peterson, the translator of *The Message*, has an interesting comment to make regarding this episode in Daniel's life:

> God has his own educational style: If we won't learn through warning, we'll learn through hard circumstances. The judgment on the king taught him how ludicrous his pretensions to majesty were. When we try to be more than human beings, we become less. In attempting to live like a god, Nebuchadnezzar lived like an animal. He only became himself again when he worshiped the God of heaven and walked humbly before him.[3]

For the king, having a troubling dream was a fairly low level of stress, as shocking as the image was. But the vision was practically nothing on the stress scale compared to the reality of a complete breakdown. Proverbs 16:18 could have been dedicated to Nebuchadnezzar: "First pride, then the crash—the bigger the ego, the harder the fall." Both Daniel and God offered a way for the king to deal with his pride, but he kept living proud until he crashed.

Stresses are like the warning dashboard lights in cars. If the issue that is causing the warning light to glow isn't addressed, the problem won't disappear. In fact, ignoring the warning light may lead to additional part failures. Stress points to a problem or a need. Surviving stress is never about ignoring it. Stress doesn't go away when we don't give it attention. It may seem to disappear, but it's only gone underground and is preparing to show up in a different way to get our attention in a more dramatic fashion.

James 1:2-5 gives us a good picture of how God uses stress in his training and education plan for us:

> Consider it a sheer gift, friends, when tests and challenges come at you from all sides. You know that under pressure, your faith-life is forced into the open and shows its true colors. So don't try to get out of anything prematurely. Let it do its work so you become mature and well-developed, not deficient in any way.
>
> If you don't know what you're doing, pray to the Father. He loves to help. You'll get his help, and won't be condescended to when you ask for it.

Stresses bring the good, the bad, and the ugly to the surface in our lives. Stresses blow the cover on areas in our lives that need work, and they also allow our better qualities to exercise their strength. Patience doesn't mean much until you are in a stressful situation that requires patience. Then you figure out quickly how full your patience tank is. Take a moment to think about a particular stressful area in your life. Got one in mind?

That didn't take long. Now, let your eyes review the James passage again and see the various action steps he mentions. Let's say the stressful issue that first came to mind for you was the pressures of poor time management. Now, as you read those verses, drop in "the pressures of poor time management" wherever appropriate. Here's what we get:

> Consider it a sheer gift, friends, when the pressures of poor time management come at you from all sides. You know that under the pressures of poor time management, your faith-life is forced into the open and shows its true colors. So don't try to get out of the pressures of poor time management prematurely. Let the pressures of poor time management do their work so you become mature and well-developed, not deficient in any way.
>
> If you don't know what you're doing, pray to the Father. He loves to help. You'll get his help, and won't be condescended to when you ask for it.

James doesn't tell us to run away from stresses; he tells us to run *toward* them. He is instructing us to face them head-on. If they require a change, that will become apparent as they force us to "become mature and well-developed." He knows that (especially at first) we are going to wonder what we're doing, so he reminds us that the frustrations of stress should drive us to God. He promises that a conversation with God in the midst of stress is like tripping a relief valve on a high pressure tank. You will feel the power that is pressing on you relax because it is being met by the power of God. This can be your experience — but it won't be unless you remember to apply this survival strategy when you find yourself under stress. God wants you to be a survivor. He's there to offer you all the help you need. So take it!

What's Worse Than Broke?
(Money Matters and Stress)

Yes, there are situations worse than being broke. Getting one-self deeply in debt with no reasonable means for repayment is worse than being broke. One of the potentially dangerous issues you're going to have to handle as you move out on your own is what to do about money. And in our society at this time in history, the issue of money has become, to a large extent, the issue of credit and debt.

If you are leaving home for the first time, you may not be far from being broke. There are two ways to stop being broke. One is to work, save, and handle your money wisely. The other is to go into debt. The first makes being broke the starting point of a productive life. The second makes being broke the first step toward slavery, stress, and an unproductive life. Realizing that you are broke is a great reality check if it drives you in the right direction. But recognize that as you live on your own, you will hear plenty of voices urging you to take the easy road and borrow your way into the easy life. If you believe that lie, it will lead you into a trap that will be difficult to escape.

If you have worked, saved money, and are using money you and/or your parents saved for college, you probably don't need this chapter. You may have already learned enough valuable lessons about money to serve you well if you keep applying them in life. As your income increases, remember that the same principles of saving, giving, investing, and thrift apply. Having more money is never a good reason to become careless with money.

We have to talk about money in a book about surviving stressful times because money matters create some of the most stressful times in people's lives. This is an amazing development in the case of Christians because God's Word includes a lot of wise advice about money. There are also many counselors available publicly who are giving sound direction to people on the basics of handling money. Everyone graduating from high school ought to listen to someone like Matt Bell before they head off to college. When people get into money trouble, one thing is always true; they have been listening to the wrong voices when it comes to money. If you don't have a specific plan about money in your life, you are a sitting target for trouble and stress.

Careless with Resources

According to Daniel 5:1, Belshazzar was the son of Nebuchadnezzar, and he shared ruling duties with his father who wasn't around much. So, young Belshazzar got to have his own way. He enjoyed the party possibilities that a king could indulge in. He seems to have been oblivious to the fact that the Medes and Persians were growing in power and were soon to conquer the Babylonian Empire. Apparently he was thinking that any consequences would arrive tomorrow and had tricked himself into believing that the settling of his accounts would always be a day away. Belshazzar was running up a huge debt of careless living and didn't take into account that the Medo-Persian bill collectors would have no mercy. It turns out that the king was living on borrowed time.

God is not a big fan of debt. We've urged you to consider creative alternatives to going into debt even when you're thinking about college expenses. And we mentioned earlier the main reason for extreme caution: Debt is a form of slavery. Proverbs 22:7 says, "The poor are always ruled over by the rich, so don't borrow and put yourself under their power." Or as another translation puts it, "The rich rule over the poor, and the borrower is servant to the lender" (NIV). One of the few places in the Bible where debt is mentioned in a positive light comes in the context of a general rule against borrowing: "Don't run up debts, except for the huge debt of love you owe each other" (Romans 13:8). Careless borrowing is spending what I don't have yet but assuming I'll have it tomorrow. Even if it turns out that I'm right and do have money tomorrow, what will I use to pay tomorrow's bills if I already spent that money yesterday? As we will see in Belshazzar's situation, debts eventually demand payment.

By chapter 5 of his book, Daniel had retired from active service in the court, and Belshazzar would probably have ignored him as an old man if he had been around. Back in Jerusalem a long time before, Daniel may have witnessed Nebuchadnezzar's soldiers carrying out the precious items from Solomon's temple and transporting them to Babylon where they were respectfully kept in the "sacred treasury" (1:2). Nebuchadnezzar was careful about not unnecessarily offending the gods of the people he conquered.

That history of respect was abandoned on the night of what turned out to be Belshazzar's last big party. As Daniel describes the event,

> King Belshazzar held a great feast for his one thousand nobles. The wine flowed freely. Belshazzar, heady with the wine, ordered that the gold and silver chalices his father Nebuchadnezzar had stolen from God's Temple of Jerusalem be brought in so that he and his nobles, his wives and concubines, could drink from them. When the gold and silver chalices were brought in, the king and his nobles, his wives and his concubines, drank wine from them. They drank the wine and drunkenly praised their gods made of gold and silver, bronze and iron, wood and stone. (5:1-4)

One of the biblical principles of healthy living is to live in the moment, not in the sense that we can do whatever we want because it pleases us at the time but in the sense that we do not need to worry about tomorrow. We need to focus on what God is doing today (see Matthew 6:34). We will look at this in greater detail in the last chapter of this book. One of the great dangers of debt is that it allows people to masquerade as if they were living in the moment. Debt makes us feel like we have the resources to do things now, but those resources don't really belong to us. Careless borrowing leads to careless living, not really counting the cost of what we are buying. Eventually, careless borrowing leads to us playing god in our lives, assuming we have more control over tomorrow than we do. Belshazzar, in a drunken stupor, thought it would be a cool new experience to misuse items that he knew were dedicated to the God of Israel as party favors in his celebration—a little like using your mom's good china for a pizza party in the basement. His value system was upside down, and the reckoning was about to come knocking at his door.

Suddenly, on the whitewashed wall in the banquet hall, the crowd witnessed the first live PowerPoint presentation in history. A large unattached hand appeared, and one of the fingers began writing script on the wall. A bold series of words flowed from the finger's movements. That stopped the show and sobered up the king in a hurry.

Belshazzar was terrified. Even he sensed this was the "handwriting on the wall" (now you know where that saying comes from). He called in all the people who were supposed to be experts at figuring out stuff like this, but they were clueless. Now the king was in a panic. But the queen (likely his grandmother) showed up and gave him some direction. She reminded him that there was someone still around who had always come through for his father in similar situations—Daniel.

The queen heard of the hysteria among the king and his nobles and came to the banquet hall. She said, "Long live the king! Don't be upset. Don't sit around looking like ghosts. There is a man in your kingdom who is full of the divine Holy Spirit. During your father's time he was well known for his intellectual brilliance and spiritual wisdom. He was so good that your father, King Nebuchadnezzar, made him the head of all the magicians, enchanters, fortunetellers, and diviners. There was no one quite like him. He could do anything — interpret dreams, solve mysteries, explain puzzles. His name is Daniel, but he was renamed Belteshazzar by the king. Have Daniel called in. He'll tell you what is going on here." (verses 10-12)

The king issued the order, and Daniel was summoned. When he arrived, Belshazzar asked Daniel to interpret the writing and promised to make him rich and famous if he could deliver the message.

Daniel politely refused the gifts but definitely delivered the message. But first he gave the young king a little history lesson about his father Nebuchadnezzar and what God had done to get his attention. He informed the king that he should have been smart enough to take a lesson from his heritage, but instead he had gone out of his way to disrespect his father's hard lessons as well as the God who taught them. Dan concluded his opening remarks with, "You used the sacred chalices to toast your gods of silver and gold, bronze and iron, wood and stone — blind, deaf, and imbecile gods. But you treat with contempt the living God who holds your entire life from birth to death in his hand" (verse 23).

Daniel used each of the words on the wall as a summary judgment on the king:

God sent the hand that wrote on the wall, and this is what is written: MENE, TEQEL, and PERES. This is what the words mean:

    Mene: God has numbered the days of your rule and they don't add up.

    Teqel: You have been weighed on the scales and you don't weigh much.

    Peres: Your kingdom has been divided up and handed over to the Medes and Persians. (verses 24–28)

That very night Belshazzar lost his kingdom and his life. His last official act was to give Daniel the promotion he didn't want and the riches he didn't need. The Medo-Persian Empire staged a bloodless takeover of a kingdom that was worse than broke in every way. Historically this was not a debt paid; this was a case in which the situation was so bad that a bankrupt king and system were prevented from the one thing they seemed bent on doing—going further into debt.

Credit Today and Tomorrow

Handling money and avoiding debt are areas in which you can definitely exercise wisdom. Recognize that there are two distinct forms of debt: secured and unsecured debt. The real dangerous ground is unsecured debt. Until recently, the best example of secured debt was a home mortgage. This kind of debt means the money borrowed is "covered" or secured by the object being bought. In other words, you may say you own the house, but as long as the mortgage is unpaid, the bank is at least part-owner of the house. If you don't pay, they sell the house and get their money back that way. Certain loans sound like secured loans, but they aren't. People borrow large amounts of money for cars, but cars don't retain value like homes do. A car has less value every day. It's not unusual for people to discover that if they get in trouble on a car loan, the money they can get from selling the car doesn't come close to paying off the loan. Suddenly they have no car and are still in debt.

The problems with money that you see all around you are mostly created by the use of unsecured debt. This is borrowing on your word to pay back not only the money you borrowed but a fee (interest) for the privilege of borrowing. Credit cards are very accessible unsecured debt to get, but the high interest rates and the subtle payment plans make them a hole you can fall into. The plan is to get you paying minimum payments each month so that you never actually pay off the debt.

As we mentioned earlier, many if not most people assume that the best way to finance an education is through debt. Often people think it's the *only* way. The plan is that large sums are borrowed in the expectation that the education will lead to a great job, which will allow the borrower to pay off the education loan quickly. But many people reach graduation with little hopes of a job and a huge debt hanging over their heads. This is major league financial stress that can take years to work out of, so do your best to avoid all or most of it. As much as possible, work your way through college. Take advantage of scholarships. Consider it a part-time job to hunt down and apply for every scrap of financial aid you can get. It will always be tempting to "just borrow the money," but the results will be hard to live with. If some of this sounds familiar, we're reinforcing thoughts from an earlier chapter because debt is a critical problem in our world today.

Being broke is stressful, but being deeply in debt is much more stressful. Being broke, as we said before, causes the right kind of stress if it motivates us to get busy earning a living. It's realizing you're in the hot desert and deciding to walk out. But handling the stress of being broke by going into debt is like feeling the heat of the desert and then jumping into a lake of quicksand. Both pictures involve a significant amount of stress, but one is definitely preferable over the other.

People who are in debt and people who want to loan you money are two groups you shouldn't be getting money advice from. Identify some people in your life who are living debt-free and ask them how they do it. They will usually be glad to share what they have learned, because most of them learned the hard way. As a general rule, when you wonder about life experiences that cause stress, talk to people who have already survived it, because they can almost always give you some pointers that will improve your own survival outlook.

You don't want to emulate Belshazzar. He may have looked like he was living large, but the stress must have been killing him. He didn't have anyone around him who was telling him the truth. One of the characteristics you want to look for in friendships throughout your life is people who will tell you the truth even if it isn't what you want to hear.

God will always tell you the truth, *especially* when it isn't something you want to hear. Isn't it interesting that one of the ways to describe our starting place when we begin a relationship with God is that we are spiritually broke? Jesus described the first step toward spiritual wealth in Matthew 5 when he said, "You're blessed when you're at the end of your rope. With less of you there is more of God and his rule" (verse 3). The traditional way to translate the phrase "end of your rope" is "poor in spirit" (NIV). It also means "spiritually bankrupt—broke." That's why we have to accept everything that God offers us (forgiveness, new life, eternal life) as a gift. There's no way we can buy it or earn it—we're spiritually broke. But admitting that fact about ourselves and opening our hands and lives to God bring his instant response. That was the whole point behind Jesus coming here to die on the cross for us, to provide for us what we could never get for ourselves: a restored and whole relationship with him. Romans 6:23 tells us, "Work hard for sin your whole life and your pension is death. But God's gift is real life, eternal life, delivered by Jesus, our Master." If you're still wondering what would motivate God to go so far out of his way for us, this is one of the verses that holds the answer: "But God put his love on the line for us by offering his Son in sacrificial death while we were of no use whatever to him" (Romans 5:8). The very worst thing compared to being broke is not knowing how much God loves you.

Who Are You When You're Alone?
(Sometimes You Can't Avoid Stress)

Neil stood for a moment on the edge of the cliff, savoring the sight. Below him was a sheer drop of seventy feet of granite. Below that, a jumbled field of car-sized boulders sloped downward hundreds of feet to the valley floor. Off to his right, through the pine trees, the lake glittered in the sun. Warm enough to release the mixed scents of pine tar and cooked leaves, the day had "fall" written all over it.

The eleven-millimeter climbing rope running through his hands reminded him this was more than just a pleasant day in the rock. That and the boisterous sounds of teenagers behind him brought him back to why he was perched on the lip of this drop-off. He was about to introduce a dozen people to the delights, challenges, and pains of rock climbing and rappelling. They had already enjoyed the scramble up through the boulder field, and several had expressed amazement over the view, the early fall colors, and the hard-edged features of this place of hewn beauty ironically called Devil's Lake State Park, in Wisconsin.

Smiling over the delight of returning to one of his favorite spots on earth, Neil realized he no longer knew how many people he had actually led to this secluded area of granite bluffs overlooking the lake. Most climbing groups stuck to the trails. This was a special place few visited, and he wanted to keep it that way.

Down at the bottom of the boulder field, he had stopped the group and told them a little about his experiences in this particular location. He let them know that one of his objectives was to always leave the area as untouched as possible. He asked the group to take note of trash and other human debris on the way up because on the way back down they would be collecting the thoughtless evidence of other people's visits to this beautiful place. The kids nodded in agreement. This was such a great adventure!

Setting up the equipment, helping each person with their climbing harnesses, teaching the basics of the sport, and then supervising the climbers kept Neil busy all day. He never got tired of assisting people through those moments of transition between the terror of standing on the edge and trying to trust the rope enough to lean back into space and the exhilaration of hanging almost weightless in the slings and pushing away from the rock face. The pattern rarely varied. Each person showed their fear in different ways, but they were all scared when it was their turn. Neil affirmed their fears. It *isn't* natural to back out over a sheer drop. The possibility of falling *should* make you nervous and focus your thoughts. But fear is not the only consideration. Trust in the instructor, facts about the equipment, and watching others do what you are about to do can all be used when dealing with fear. But the moment of truth is always when you're the one standing on the edge with space behind you, the drop below you, and a dry mouth. Each person had to overcome those feelings in order to experience the delight of the trust payoff. The group had a great day. Every one of them now had a personal example of faith — trusting what you know enough to pass through your fears and take the step.

Late in the afternoon, as he packed up the equipment, Neil smiled again, filled with contentment over a day well spent. From the top of his pack he pulled out several large plastic bags he was going to pass out to the group so they could pick up the trash on the way down through the boulder field. He shouldered the pack and then walked back along the cliff to the point where he could begin to descend with the kids. As he looked back one last time to that favorite spot, he was stunned by what he saw. It took him a moment to take in what had occurred. While Neil had been focused on keeping each climber safe, talking them through their fears, other members of the group had taken sharp rocks and scraped and gouged their names and the date onto the faces of several boulders above the climb. Despite his words about the beauty of that location and the years of efforts to keep it unspoiled, people he had brought to this place had marred it. Not willing to let others experience something wonderful in the same way they were privileged to experience it, several people had to announce to others, "I was here first and I made sure you won't be able to enjoy it as much as I did."

It took years of rain, wind, and ice to gradually wipe out those ugly scars. For Neil, his adventure, filled with such delight and beauty, was tainted by the disappointment, anger, and shame he felt knowing the kids had defaced something he valued so highly. What shocked Neil the most was that the people with him hadn't stopped long enough to think about how what they were about to do would affect others. All they could see was what they wanted to do in that moment when no one who might express a different thought was looking.

The Question

Who are you when no one is watching? If you think about that question for a little while, it will probably cause some stress. At this point in your life, you may feel like you rarely have moments in your life when *someone* isn't watching. If it isn't parents, it's teachers and coaches—not to mention principals, police officers, and friends. If you live and drive in a large city, you are probably recorded on traffic cameras several times each day. But the question is still valid: Who are you when no one is watching? It comes up in many ways. How does a parent's presence affect your behavior? Do you drive differently when you know there's video surveillance of an intersection or a police car with the speed gun pointed at you? How do different combinations of friends affect the way you act and speak? We do adapt to different situations. And yet, somewhere in the middle of all the role playing there's the real you. Do you know who that is? To get a clue, think about the way you are and what you do when no one is watching. And perhaps more to the point, given how often others observe us, in what ways are you always the same person, no matter who is watching?

You may be thinking, *I'm always the same person, whether or not someone is watching.* But you may also be feeling some guilt over the things you think or do when no one else is around. Is there something you're hiding? Does it cause you some panic to think of someone else discovering who you are when you're alone? How do you feel when you think about God knowing your every thought and action? The guilt, sorrow, and fear you feel at the thought of others knowing the real you is evidence of self-imposed stress in your life.

Our friend Daniel lived his life in patterns. He was free to improvise and be creative because he preserved certain basics of his lifestyle that gave him structure and direction. These repetitions gave his life a healthy rhythm. And the most important of these was the regularity of his conversations with God. Three times each day — morning, noon, and evening — Daniel excused himself and spent time in prayer. He talked to God at other times, and he certainly turned to God in stressful times, but day in and day out, like clockwork, Daniel's routine included a habit of prayer. He didn't force others to imitate him and he didn't make a big deal of his time alone with God, but he was consistent.

What are the positive patterns in your life? What habits are ingrained? Do you floss daily? How often do you shower? When do you check and change the oil in your car? How regular is your pattern of church attendance? In what repeated ways is God a part of your daily routine? As you move out on your own, realize that the best way to preserve that newfound sense of freedom is to choose wisely the habits and actions that will shape your life. If you don't choose the patterns for your life, others will choose them for you. The world around you has a definite and destructive set of habits it will gladly impose on you if you aren't paying attention. How else can we explain the creeping despair in people who spend every Friday night getting drunk, cope with the weekend in a stupor, and then suffer through Monday with a hangover, claiming all the while that they had a great weekend, even though they can't really point to anything specific that made it great?

Perhaps a better way to think about the patterns in your life right now is to ask the question, Twenty years from now, what do I want to be the central characteristics of my life? Whatever will really be worth having in your life two decades from now is worth building into your life right now. If you want to have a mature yet growing relationship with God, then work on it now. If you want your life to be marked by health, integrity, and contentment, practice these personal disciplines now. If you want your relationships with others to be positive, learn what it takes now and start treating people that way. The people in your life right now might not still be there twenty years from now, but treating them as you want to be treated will prepare you for relationships to come.

When the famous prayer incident happened in Daniel's life, he had already had a long and successful career as a counselor to kings. By the time Darius came along and took over Babylon, Daniel had such a reputation for integrity, wisdom, and leadership that Darius made him his first adviser, with power second only to the king himself. Daniel didn't apply for this job, but the king made him one of the three men supervising the 120 governors who managed Darius's kingdom.

The king's favor toward Daniel didn't sit well with the other leaders. They didn't like Darius's arrangement, and they resented Daniel's leadership. He was not a part of their network of power and manipulation.

> The vice-regents and governors got together to find some old scandal or skeleton in Daniel's life that they could use against him, but they couldn't dig up anything. He was totally exemplary and trustworthy. They could find no evidence of negligence or misconduct. So they finally gave up and said, "We're never going to find anything against this Daniel unless we can cook up something religious." (Daniel 6:4-5)

The strategy they came up with is as old (or recent) as politics itself. If you can't find something negative about a person, create a situation that looks bad and destroy the person that way.

When they approached Darius, the conspirators presented their statement as the unanimous counsel from all of them, but Daniel was conspicuously absent. Their words were designed to appeal to the king's vanity. They recommended that the king issue a decree that for thirty days no one could pray to any god or man but the king, and those who did not would be thrown into a den of lions. Apparently Darius only heard the part about everyone praying to him for thirty days. He probably thought about how honoring that would be. It didn't occur to him that someone might have a legitimate reason for *not* praying to him. This was a double setup. Both Daniel and the king were "played" into being on opposite sides. The conspirators must have figured that Darius's anger over Daniel's deliberate violation of a law of the Medes and Persians would protect them from any fallout over manipulating the king.

By the time Daniel got the memo about the new law, it was too late to argue his case. He simply continued his long practice of praying three times at home by a window that faced west, toward Jerusalem. It wasn't difficult for the conspirators to catch him in the act of breaking the law. And they immediately brought the case before the king, reminding him that the unconditional law was in place and that anyone disregarding it was subject to a visit to the lions' den. They still failed to mention the identity of the accused. It wasn't until the king agreed he had indeed created the law and decreed the punishment that he was told the first person to be punished under the new law would be his trusted adviser Daniel. Darius's response tells us a lot about the stresses of this situation:

> At this, the king was very upset and tried his best to get Daniel out of the fix he'd put him in. He worked at it the whole day long.

> But then the conspirators were back: "Remember, O king, it's the law of
> the Medes and Persians that the king's decree can never be changed."
>
> The king caved in and ordered Daniel brought and thrown into the lions'
> den. But he said to Daniel, "Your God, to whom you are so loyal, is going to get
> you out of this." (verses 14–16)

How different this was from the earlier situation between
the three friends and King Nebuchadnezzar. In the first case,
the king arrogantly assumed that his edict to send the men to
the furnace was beyond the help of any god. But Darius decided
the only solution to the predicament his own officials had
created was to apply the law to Daniel and let God keep him
safe. Daniel's consistency over his lifetime as an honest,
God-fearing man was the witness needed for the king to make
the leap of trusting God's power. This might have been vastly
different had Daniel not been the man he appeared to be.

The sentence was carried out late in the day. The lions' den
was sealed, and it appeared to everyone that so was Daniel's
fate. No one really expected him to survive the night with the
cats. Daniel was alone.

We have no idea what Daniel was actually feeling in those
moments before he was lowered into the lions' den. He had
been doing what was his private practice for a lifetime, yet it
was suddenly being used against him. His daily time with God
seemed for the moment to have led to nothing. It would be safe
to think that Daniel was under stress. But there is no record that
he pleaded for his life or outwardly expressed any concern. He
must have known it wouldn't make any difference. At least

Daniel could rest in the knowledge that he had not brought this stress upon himself by hiding something for the other leaders to dig up about him.

Just in case you haven't noticed yet, don't expect that life will ever be stress-free. The lesson of Daniel's life, as is the case for so many of the people who have served God most faithfully, is that God does not plan for us to figure out life and then coast into the sunset. The Bible is filled with parallel examples. Joseph suffered repeated setbacks before he finally saw the dream of his childhood fulfilled, but he was never free from stress. Moses lived a life of escalating stress until he stood looking from the mountaintop at the Promised Land he would not enter. Esther endured the stress of having to risk everything to save her people.

The real test of whether God is with you isn't the number of stress-free moments you have each day. Some days will be saturated with stress; others will be smooth sailing. We know God is with us when we experience his presence, no matter what our stress level is at the moment. King David, no stranger to stressful situations (and plenty that he didn't handle quite right), wrote the best-known psalm in which he compared his relationship with God to a sheep's connection with a shepherd.

The first lines of that psalm are all about stress-free living:

> Goᴅ, my shepherd!
>> I don't need a thing.
> You have bedded me down in lush meadows,

> you find me quiet pools to drink from.
> True to your word,
> > you let me catch my breath
> > and send me in the right direction. (Psalm 23:1-3)

Sheep are not fans of stress. They require a lot of care from the shepherd. But even the most thoughtful shepherd can't keep all stress from the lives of his sheep. Sometimes, the sheep step right into it! But David remembered that something very special happened in times of stress:

> Even when the way goes through
> > Death Valley,
> I'm not afraid
> > when you walk at my side.
> Your trusty shepherd's crook
> > makes me feel secure.

> You serve me a six-course dinner
> > right in front of my enemies.
> You revive my drooping head;
> > my cup brims with blessing.

> Your beauty and love chase after me
> > every day of my life.
> I'm back home in the house of GOD
> > for the rest of my life. (verses 4-6)

God doesn't leave us when the stress is on; he actually comes closer. If we are paying attention, he will walk at our side through the darkest valley. Ultimately, the art of surviving stressful times boils down to the company we keep. Daniel kept company with God—wherever he was. That's who he was, someone in touch with God whether or not anyone was watching. For us, it is never a waste of time to keep asking, "When I'm alone, at peace, or under stress, how much of my attention is drawn to God and what he means to me?" As embarrassing as it might be, who we are and what we do when we think no one is watching is pretty close to who we really are!

Back in the Den

We don't know if they kept the lights on in the lions' den after they locked the door with Daniel inside. There was no guarantee that Daniel would be spared the role of lion appetizer, but just as his three friends recognized when they faced the furnace, Daniel knew God was with him—and that awareness was even more important than surviving.

So, while Daniel had a pajama party with Simba and kin (apparently he wasn't allergic to cat hair), the king had a terrible night. He didn't eat. He was worried about Daniel, and probably ticked that he had been tricked into signing his trusted adviser's death warrant. Daniel was the only person he knew who wouldn't have pulled the kind of devious tactic the others in his court had pulled. The conspirators underestimated the connection Daniel had with Darius. They may not have realized it yet, but their fate was sealed.

In the morning, when the king showed up to check on Daniel, he shouted into the pit, "Daniel, servant of the living God, has your God, whom you serve so loyally, saved you from the lions?" (Daniel 6:20). Pause the tape for just a moment. The boy from Jerusalem had come a long way. He had made an impression on the highest level of government. The king of the Medo-Persian Empire was so hoping that Daniel was safe that he was willing to recognize the living God as well as Daniel's ultimate allegiance to his God. Daniel had proven to his friend, the king, that in a showdown of commitment, Daniel would side with God even though he remained a faithful counselor of the king. King Darius may not have been ready to surrender to the living God himself, but he didn't see a problem with Daniel serving that God. He knew from experience that Daniel was the kind of person he was because of his relationship with God.

If you were Daniel, wouldn't you have waited just a moment to answer the king's yell? Maybe he took a second to think through what he was going to say while he had the king's shocked attention. "O king, live forever! . . . My God sent his angel, who closed the mouths of the lions so that they would not hurt me. I've been found innocent before God and also before you, O king. I've done nothing to harm you" (verses 21-22). Daniel complimented the king, claimed his innocence, and stated his case. Finally! The rush to judgment had been so swift that Daniel hadn't been given a chance to speak for himself.

The conspirators gambled a lot to take down Daniel. And

they lost big-time. Not only were they ushered into the lions' den in Daniel's place, but their wives and children were sent in to join them. Not having been fed the night before, the lions were understandably famished and made fast food out of Dan's enemies. The king was in no mood to listen to excuses and explanations. He resented being made an accessory to the attempted murder of Daniel.

Once Darius tipped the scales of justice back to even, he went an unexpected step beyond. He insisted on making an official statement about Daniel's God. He stopped short of saying Daniel's God was now his God, but he did encourage all of his subjects to consider seriously the God whom Daniel served. His announcement sounds an awful lot like one of the Jewish psalms about God. Perhaps Darius had Daniel draft the order for him to sign!

King Darius published this proclamation to every race, color, and creed on earth:

Peace to you! Abundant peace!
>   I decree that Daniel's God shall be worshiped and feared in all parts
>   of my kingdom.
>   He is the living God, world without end. His kingdom never falls.
>   His rule continues eternally.
>   He is a savior and rescuer.
>   He performs astonishing miracles in heaven and on earth.
>   He saved Daniel from the power of the lions. (verses 25–27)

We know that genuine spirituality can't be legislated (though some have tried). We can be invited, encouraged, and even pleaded with to worship and fear the true God, but no one can force us to follow through if we are not willing. We might be willing to put on a little charade in public and make people think we believe and obey God, but who we are in private, when no one is looking (other than God), will reveal who we really are.

Being accused unfairly and even judged unfairly will naturally bring a tsunami of stress into our lives. Our instinctive human response is to immediately begin plotting revenge. Daniel left all that in God's hands. He handled the stress of the moment by keeping his attention first on the God he had always served, and second, on the king into whose service his God had placed him. From Daniel's perspective, there wasn't anything else worth worrying about. Stuff like injustice and vengeance he left in God's hands. His life demonstrates that God handled that part of things with no problem.

10

Tomorrow, Tomorrow
(Stress and Forever)

Tomorrow made it into a Bond film with the title *Tomorrow Never Dies*, although it's a little hard to figure out what the title has to do with the story line. *Tomorrow* was also the key word in a hit song from the musical *Annie*. That tune made some interesting observations about the nature of tomorrow. First is a somewhat hopeful promise that the sun will shine tomorrow, something we know to be true even if it's a cloudy day and we can't see the sun. And then there is the reminder that tomorrow is always a day away. Which is not a way of saying tomorrow never dies but of saying tomorrow never comes. Just about the time that tomorrow arrives, it changes into today. And tomorrow is still, as the little girl sang, a day away.

Jesus also made some interesting observations about tomorrow in the broader context of worry. Worry is one of the undercover disguises of stress. We may not recognize the stress at first, but we can sure recognize the worry. Jesus showed us that if we can learn to deal with worry, we will also be able to deal with stress. Let's look at the thoughts he included in a longer passage that most of us know as the Sermon on the Mount:

If you decide for God, living a life of God-worship, it follows that you don't fuss about what's on the table at mealtimes or whether the clothes in your closet are in fashion. There is far more to your life than the food you put in your stomach, more to your outer appearance than the clothes you hang on your body. Look at the birds, free and unfettered, not tied down to a job description, careless in the care of God. And you count far more to him than birds.

Has anyone by fussing in front of the mirror ever gotten taller by so much as an inch? All this time and money wasted on fashion — do you think it makes that much difference? Instead of looking at the fashions, walk out into the fields and look at the wildflowers. They never primp or shop, but have you ever seen color and design quite like it? The ten best-dressed men and women in the country look shabby alongside them.

If God gives such attention to the appearance of wildflowers — most of which are never even seen — don't you think he'll attend to you, take pride in you, do his best for you? What I'm trying to do here is to get you to relax, to not be so preoccupied with *getting*, so you can respond to God's *giving*. People who don't know God and the way he works fuss over these things, but you know both God and how he works. Steep your life in God-reality, God-initiative, God-provisions. Don't worry about missing out. You'll find all your everyday human concerns will be met.

Give your entire attention to what God is doing right now, and don't get worked up about what may or may not happen tomorrow. God will help you deal with whatever hard things come up when the time comes. (Matthew 6:25-34)

Almost everything we have talked about in this book is included in this brief statement by Jesus. It shows us that he really understands exactly how we are wired and what works best for us. As you read over it, note that terms like *fuss over* and *preoccupied* are synonyms for *worry*. He was reminding us that one of the dependable clues that things are not right between us and God is when worry and stress rear their ugly heads.

If you read and apply that passage every day for a month, it would transform your life. Your priorities would change, your relationship with God and with others would be altered, and stress would take on a different role in your life.

A variety of stressors will arise in the coming months and years that you can apply this verse to. When your roommate comes home from shopping with a whole new wardrobe, you might feel like what fills your own closet is inadequate. A professor might rant and rave over a classmate's brilliant term paper, and you're looking at the large C circled in the top corner of the paper you spent the whole semester preparing. You've been invited to a party, but you don't know anyone who's going, except for the popular kid who asked you to come, and you wonder if compared to him anyone will want to talk to you. A meeting with your adviser is coming up, and you have no idea what you want to do with your life, let alone what major to choose and classes to take. Your first day of school is next week, and you wonder how you will ever make friends like the ones you left back home.

The passage in Matthew 6 will give you some great reasons

not to stress out about the future. Basically, when we let current and future events create stress for us, that's a clue that we are not trusting God enough. We are taking things into our own hands that fit only in his hands. So, inviting stress is letting the overwhelming overwhelm us. And once stress is overwhelming us, it's hard to get out from under it.

Briefly, these verses also give us at least five activities that will undermine and gradually eliminate stress from our lives. First, look at the birds. God takes care of them; he'll take care of you. Simple? Yes. Profound? Definitely. So when your car breaks down and you've got ten minutes to get to your off-campus job, remember that God will provide. Second, look at the flowers. God lavishes creativity on them though they only last for days. God designed you for eternity with him; he will definitely care for his investment. When you look at the variety of people on your campus and begin to feel inadequate in your intelligence, appearance, athletic ability, creativity, or plans for the future, keep in mind that each of you was designed by God. Third, focus on what God is doing more than on anything else. That's where the exciting things are happening—lives being changed, hope renewed, miracles occurring. Praise him when the guy across the hall finally comes to Bible study with you after you've invited him for five months. Rejoice when the Christian groups on campus join together to worship the Savior. Fourth, live your life for God ("Steep your life in God-reality, God-initiative, God-provisions") because that's what life is supposed to be about anyway! And fifth, live today. That's all you will ever have. Tomorrow never comes. Even in eternity, it will always be today. Today is where and when you meet with and walk with God. Why would you want to waste time stressing about tomorrow? When it becomes today, God will be with you.

Ultimately, the key to surviving whatever stress you face in life will involve your relationship with God. Let him get that right in you, and everything else will work itself out. Or, as Jesus put it, "God will help you deal with whatever hard things come up when the time comes."

NOTES

1. Eugene Peterson, *The Invitation* (Colorado Springs, CO: NavPress, 2008), 92–93.
2. Gilbert K. Chesterton, *Orthodoxy* (New York: John Lane Co., 1908), 152, emphasis added.
3. Eugene Peterson, *Conversations: The Message with Its Translator* (Colorado Springs, CO: NavPress, 2007), 1348.

THOUGHTS/REFLECTIONS

THOUGHTS/REFLECTIONS

THOUGHTS/REFLECTIONS

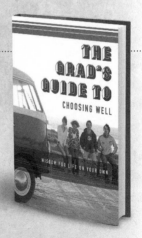

MY LIFE IS **TOUGHER** THAN MOST **PEOPLE REALIZE.**

I TRY TO KEEP EVERYTHING IN BALANCE: FRIENDS, FAMILY, WORK, SCHOOL, AND GOD.

IT'S NOT EASY.

I KNOW WHAT MY PARENTS BELIEVE AND WHAT MY PASTOR SAYS.

BUT IT'S NOT ABOUT THEM. IT'S ABOUT ME...

ISN'T IT TIME I OWN MY FAITH?

THROUGH THICK AND THIN, KEEP YOUR HEARTS AT ATTENTION, IN ADORATION BEFORE CHRIST, YOUR MASTER. BE READY TO SPEAK UP AND TELL ANYONE WHO ASKS WHY YOU'RE LIVING THE WAY YOU ARE, AND ALWAYS WITH THE UTMOST COURTESY. 1 PETER 3:15 (MSG)